Joseph Healy and **David Hornery**
co-founders of Judo Bank

-

A masterclass for start-ups
and entrepreneurs

Black Belt

MACMILLAN

Praise for *Black Belt*

'Enjoy the ride and the read, through euphoria and despair, joy and heartbreak. There's no more important task for the world's future than to groom more entrepreneurs. If you're going to be one of them, consider *Black Belt* your go-to guide.'
John Mullins | Associate Professor of Management Practice, London Business School; author, *Break the Rules! The six counter-conventional mindsets that can help anyone change the world*

'A must-read for all aspiring entrepreneurs seeking to develop start-ups or restructure their existing businesses.'
Paul Constantinou AM | Founder, Quest Apartment Hotels

'The founders of Judo Bank have over 70 years of combined international banking experience, but they had to completely rethink their approach to banking to turn an idea into a remarkable story. While banking is the backdrop, the problems they faced will resonate with all entrepreneurs and the lessons in the way they wrestled with the challenges of creating, launching and spectacularly growing a start-up make this an absolute gem of a book for any aspiring entrepreneur.'
Colin McLeod | Professor, Faculty of Business and Economics, the University of Melbourne; Executive Director, Melbourne Entrepreneurial Centre

'It's not often you get founders and entrepreneurs who actually talk about their success with equal focus on their near misses and their abundance of challenges. The best way to know what's ahead of you, if you are in a start-up or a business facing challenges, is to read about someone else's challenges and study how they reacted, responded, pivoted and never gave up. That's what *Black Belt* is all about. This is a great read.'
Mark Bouris AM | Founder and Chairman, Wizard Home Loans

'*Black Belt* contains a wealth of sage advice and keen insights, distilled from the authors' inspiring firsthand account of the creation of Judo Bank. This book can serve as a valuable and practical guide for aspirant change-makers. For me, what sets this excellent book apart from similar ones is its strong focus on fundamentals of business strategy and ensuring their integration into the entrepreneurial journey.'
Steven Maguire | Professor of Strategy, Innovation and Entrepreneurship, the University of Sydney Business School

'Joseph and David lavishly open their own vaults of knowledge, experience and wisdom and share priceless, hands-on and pragmatic insights, advice and guidance. *Black Belt* is a must-read material for every business student, entrepreneur, industry professional and corporate leader aspiring to create a better, just, ethical and moral world. This book sincerely deserves a place in every business school's library.'
Dr Dimitrios Salampasis (MAICD) | Director, Master of Financial Technologies, Swinburne University of Technology; fintech capability leader

Joseph: To my son George, who tragically died in 2021. I miss him so much.

David: For Bron, my soulmate, and Georgie, Sash and Ellie, the lights of my life.

Your authors

Joseph Healy, co-founder, Judo Bank

Joseph is a 35-plus-year career banker with a broad background across most aspects of banking. He started his career at Lloyds Bank in London, followed by a long stint at Citibank (mainly in London) and then Canadian bank CIBC World Markets. He joined ANZ Bank in 1998 and National Australia Bank (NAB) in late 2006, leaving in late 2014. He then took a year sabbatical at a university in Ningbo, China, during which time he started working with David on what today is Judo Bank. He is the author of three books: *Corporate Governance and Shareholder Wealth Creation* (2003), *Chinese Firms Going Global: Can They Succeed?* (2018) and *Breaking the Banks* (2019).

David Hornery, co-founder, Judo Bank

David is also a 35-year veteran of the banking sector, beginning in the financial markets and investment banking before moving into commercial banking. He started out in 1986 at two broking houses – GB Nathan and Potter Partners – before moving to Macquarie Bank and spending 11 years in their Financial Markets division. Then he moved across to ANZ, spending seven years as Global Head of Capital Markets and four years in Singapore as CEO of ANZ Asia. He moved to NAB in 2008, stepping out in 2015 to work with Joseph on Judo Bank. Outside banking, David is Non Executive Chair of Studio THI (formerly The Hornery Institute), a not-for-profit that contributes to the global dialogue on community formation and place making and urban change preparedness within communities.

First published in 2023 by Major Street Publishing Pty Ltd

First published in India 2024 by Macmillan
an imprint of Pan Macmillan Publishing India Private Limited
707 Kailash Building
26 K. G. Marg, New Delhi 110001
www.panmacmillan.co.in

Pan Macmillan, The Smithson, 6 Briset Street, Farringdon, London EC1M 5NR
Associated companies throughout the world
www.panmacmillan.com

ISBN 978-93-6113-920-8

1 3 5 7 9 8 6 4 2

Internal design by Production Works
Printed in India by Gopsons Papers Pvt. Ltd., Noida

Contents

1 **Introduction**
Setting the scene 1

2 **'Project Greengate'**
Our entrepreneurial journey begins 13

3 **Measure twice, cut once**
From vision to business case 37

4 **The plan of attack**
Competitive advantage and the ability to scale 53

5 **Dodging blows**
Pitfalls to avoid 71

6 **Hearts, minds and money**
Securing investors 81

7 **Finding our balance**
Building the team and culture 109

8 **How to reach black belt**
Ten lessons we learnt 145

9 **The challenger mindset**
Maintaining founder centrism 165

10 **Sharing our start-up with the world**
Taking Judo public 179

Final reflections 185
References 187
Index 192

1
Introduction
Setting the scene

Many years ago, one of your authors was reading a guide on doing a PhD. The guide succinctly summarised the task ahead: doing a bachelor's degree was a general education, a master's degree was a licence to practice, and a PhD was a licence to teach. In many ways, after seven years of hard work building Judo Bank (along with others), this book is our PhD on how to build a new business in a complex industry in a way that is scalable and potentially industry-transformative. It is also a book about maintaining a start-up's biggest cultural asset as it grows: a founder or owner mindset.

Our motivation in writing this book is largely to pass on insights and advice that might assist others, as our journey was, in turn, greatly assisted by the advice and insights that others provided to us. We do not pretend to be the font of all knowledge here – as you will see, we have made our share of missteps along the way – but we do hope that you will benefit or gain insight from our experience and real-world learnings, successes and mistakes alike. Vicariously learning from other people's mistakes can be just as powerful (and a lot less painful) than learning from one's own experience, if you know how to learn!

WeWork is a wonderful example of this, as is the demise of Greensill Capital, both of which we explore later in the book.

We were also motivated by what we see as a potentially transformational decade ahead. Having come late in our careers to the entrepreneurial economy, we are now big believers that the most valuable and interesting businesses in the coming years will be those built by entrepreneurs. The global pools of private and venture capital have never been deeper or more broadly available, and the technological tools available are more powerful, flexible and affordable. We also believe that there are many latent entrepreneurs of all ages who, with a little bit of encouragement, could take the leap to begin a new and more exciting phase of their careers. This book is largely motivated by, and dedicated to, those who have that same flickering of entrepreneurial ambition that we and our fellow co-founders – Chris Bayliss, Tim Alexander, Kate Keenan and Alex Twigg – had back in late 2015.

Unlike numerous books written about start-ups, this book has been written by practitioners. This is a real-world story written by those who have been squarely at the coalface, and who have learnt that, without a clear vision, sense of purpose, self-belief, capacity for hard work, limitless resilience and appetite for risk-taking, dreams of business success will likely be nothing more than just that: dreams.

Many would-be entrepreneurs struggle to move past the dream stage, because they do not know how to turn those dreams into viable and scalable businesses. Even when they are successful in building a business, burning questions can often remain: *Could this have been an even bigger and better business? Why didn't we lay the foundations for scale? Why weren't we more visionary, more ambitious?*

This book is firmly based on making dreams (or visions) happen by laying down some basic principles as a foundation for entrepreneurs to build on. 'Measure twice, cut once' is a theme or mantra that will reoccur throughout this book; we are not advocating the 'just do it' school of entrepreneurship. Such an approach, while appealing to the entrepreneurial animal spirit, can bring chaos and is a major reason why so many start-ups fail. To quote HL Mencken: 'There is always a well-known solution to every human problem – neat, plausible, and wrong'. A more disciplined and focused management approach, such as that detailed in this book, will not necessarily guarantee success; however, it will significantly reduce the number of risks that result in failure by highlighting many of the trapdoors and trip-wires that can exist. This book will also hopefully help you understand and balance the two emotions that are a feature of the roller-coaster nature of start-ups: euphoria and despair.

How this book is organised

We have structured the book into ten chapters:

- In **Chapter 1**, we set the scene for this book.
- In **Chapter 2**, we describe some of our early thinking and experiences.
- In **Chapter 3**, we describe our process of turning a vision into a business case capable of withstanding investor, regulator and prospective-employee scrutiny. This is arguably the most important part of the journey, and is where our philosophy of 'measure twice, cut once' was brought to life. This was a tortuous process, but we hope it makes for a highly informative read!
- In **Chapter 4**, we emphasise the importance of having a competitive advantage underpinning the business. There is little point coming to market with a proposition that fails to differentiate itself in a sustainable way.
- In **Chapter 5**, we highlight some of the common pitfalls that entrepreneurs face when thinking about competitive advantage and culture.

- **Chapter 6** is where the rubber hits the road, or where the PowerPoint becomes something much more. We describe the journey of raising the all-important seed capital, regulatory engagement, assembling the founder team, the many people we met along the way and the good advice that we received, so much of which became powerfully evident to us in the years after receiving it.
- In **Chapter 7**, we describe the approach to building the broader team and shaping the culture within the business. This process is pivotal to the future of the business, going into the breadth, depth and strength of the 'concrete' that provides the foundation of the company. It is where some big mistakes can be made (and were, in our case). We also touch on the importance of mental and physical health, given the huge demands that are placed on the leadership team when the risk of failure remains a possibility.
- In **Chapter 8**, we consolidate the lessons we learnt and the mistakes that we made, including the occasion when we put most of our eggs in the one basket hoping that a particular investor would come through. We highlight the importance of listening to your people – and not through annual employee surveys, which are about as reflective of people's genuine views as elections in places like Zimbabwe. And, while it may feel off-topic at first, we also talk about ageism and how it creates a psychological barrier to many would-be entrepreneurs when it should not.
- In **Chapter 9,** we highlight a major trap that growth businesses can sleepwalk into when the twin evils of bureaucracy and complexity creep into the business and how (and why) the concept of a 'founder-centric' culture is so important for combating them.
- Finally, in **Chapter 10**, we talk through the journey of listing Judo Bank on the public equity market and the pros and cons

of doing so. It is not a decision to be taken lightly, even though many young companies rush into it (and often regret doing so). We link this journey back to the concept of founder centrism and how it is so important when navigating the inevitable transitions that entering the public market causes in on a company. As a company becomes public and the business continues to grow, some of the original founders may leave and new executives join, which makes maintaining a founder mindset challenging.

Defining a start-up

Two definitions will be helpful in reading this book: those of 'start-up' and 'entrepreneur'.

Start-up

There are many definitions of 'start-up', but we like the simple one that says that a start-up is a new business initiative undertaken by one or more entrepreneurs with the intention of developing and validating a scalable business model. We think it is helpful to adopt the distinction that Peter Thiel suggests in his book *Zero to One: Notes on Startups, or How to Build the Future* between a start-up in an already established product market, where the new entrant is bringing more of what is familiar (Thiel calls this a '1 to n start-up'), and a start-up that creates something brand new (which Thiel calls a '0 to 1 start-up'). Regardless, though, all start-ups face a high level of risk and uncertainty – hence, the failure rate is high.

Entrepreneur

Again, there are many definitions of 'entrepreneur'. The classic one is that an entrepreneur is an individual who creates a new business, bearing most of the early risk and enjoying material rewards if the business is successful. What all entrepreneurs have in common is a set of personal traits: they are always abundant thinkers, driven by passion and purpose, courageous when it comes to their personal risk appetite, and excited by the idea of being a founder of a new business that could shape an industry.

We include in our definition 'intrapreneurs', who are entrepreneurially minded but operate within established businesses as employees. They are often responsible for creating new lines of business, but in any material or practical sense don't really bear much risk or, therefore, reward relative to their talents. As we discuss in Chapter 7, particularly in large organisations, these individuals often succumb to the organisational 'immune system' response to change and innovation: search and destroy. Therefore, it is not unusual for them to seek management buyouts (MBOs) of the businesses they have played a lead role in creating, or to go on and launch their own businesses.

Sobering facts

The market for a book like this is based on two sets of facts.

First, new businesses or start-ups are critical to future economic vibrancy. The success of economies in the future will largely be determined by the entrepreneurial drive and skills of thousands of individuals with a vision and with real drive to make things happen. As Chris Zook and James Allen put it in their book *The Founder's Mentality,* we are facing 'a future that more than ever rewards speed, open-mindedness, human motivation, and adaptability'.

Second, and soberingly, most start-ups fail or cease to exist in their own right, including three of the four new Australian banks licensed in 2019. Conversely, however, a few can become unicorns (businesses valued at over $1 billion) – there are several start-ups in Australia that have achieved this status, including Judo Bank. Some achieve this quickly and some over time, but globally there are more and more every year.

Regarding start-up failure rates, here are some statistics to reflect on (from a 2022 *Moneyzine* article):

- 42% of start-up businesses failed because there is no market need for their services or products.
- 29% failed because they ran out of cash.
- 23% failed because they didn't have the right team running the business.
- 19% were outcompeted.
- 18% failed because of pricing and cost issues.
- 17% failed because of a poor product offering.
- 17% failed because they lacked a business model.
- 14% failed because of poor marketing.
- 14% failed because they ignored their customers.

The truth is that there are hundreds of statistics on start-up failures, some showing that as many as nine out of ten start-ups will fail. The point is that, when you start a new business, there is a much higher chance of failure than there is of success. Despite what the statistics might say, however, failure is rarely the product of one thing going wrong: it is usually the product of multiple things going wrong. Failure is also more of a slow-motion affair than a sudden car crash: it rarely happens quickly.

One of the difficulties in getting a clear understanding of why start-ups fail is what psychologists call 'fundamental attribution error'. Entrepreneurs often have a cognitive bias to assume their own failure was down to reasons outside their control, such as changing market conditions or sheer bad luck, while attributing failure in others to their lack of preparation, inexperienced management, weak funding plan or aggressive risk-taking – in other words, their character or personality.

Harvard Business School Professor Thomas Eisenmann spent 24 years studying why start-ups fail and wrote an excellent book on the subject. He found that most start-ups don't succeed, and more than two-thirds never deliver a return above their cost of capital.

This is sobering indeed, but the odds can be changed: there are tried, tested and practical ways to increase the prospect of success at both the outset and through the various build phases. We felt that there was an important contribution to be made in telling our story and providing our perspective on how to shift the odds, how we navigated the many icebergs – some visible, many not – that litter the stormy waters of building a new business.

While this book is very much framed by the story of the creation of Judo Bank, it is peppered with insights and advice relevant to any new business. In using our story as the case study, our goal is to bring these insights to life in a real and meaningful way, and to highlight how good management and entrepreneurship can go hand in hand. We believe the stories that captivate people and enrich understanding are those that are true to the teller, the audience and, importantly, the moment or situation. So, in our story, we have stayed true to the events and experiences, with no exaggeration or avoidance of mentioning rookie mistakes. In fact, in many ways those errors – and the learnings derived from them – are every bit as important as the successes. This is an accurate account of our experiences and insights, warts and all.

We would add that, as veteran bankers, we have seen literally thousands upon thousands of businesses succeed, drift and fail over the years. We have come to a belief that, assuming a given business opportunity is viable, it is the business' *management* that fails far more frequently than the business itself: management failure causes business failure. This is a subtle but important distinction. During the COVID-19 crisis, some businesses languished, while others in the same sector did not. Why? We saw clearly during COVID-19 that many well-managed businesses used the crisis as an opportunity to rethink their business models and accelerate thinking on aspects such as digitalisation and new channels. This was particularly aided in Australia during the first phase of the pandemic by the substantial nature of the federal government support package. As *The Economist* noted in a very thoughtful article, 'The pandemic could give way to an era of rapid productivity growth'. Equally there were many organisations that did not respond and take the opportunity.

Of course, COVID-19 impacted some businesses – particularly the young and small – in a way that they could do little about; but, to be clear, we see these as the minority. The difference between those that didn't waste the crisis and those that did is management.

What to expect from this book

In the book, we cover multiple challenges and learnings of business-building.

One key theme is the challenge of raising capital. Through building Judo Bank, we came to know how the international private capital investor market works. As we discuss in Chapter 6, we wore out a lot of shoe leather travelling around the world meeting with potential investors – close to 100, in fact – before we got our first investment. Our experience is very consistent with what Paul Gompers et al. wrote in an excellent *Harvard Business Review* article called 'How Venture Capitalists Make Decisions'. In that article, which was based on research involving almost 900 investors, the authors made several observations that are consistent with our experience:

- Access to an investor network is critical to getting funding.
- Investors will look at over 100 deals for every one they invest in.
- The strength of the founding team, more than the business model, is a key determinant of the decision to invest.

- The favoured financial metric is the annualised internal rate of return (IRR), which was often based on an IPO or other exit event expectation rather than a more traditional discounted cash flow (DCF) analysis.

The research highlighted that of 100 opportunities shown to investors, 28 result in a meeting and fewer than five result in due diligence, with one resulting in an actual investment. The research also revealed that a typical deal takes 83 days to close.

A particularly interesting insight from the research, and one that we dive into further in the book, is the third point above: many investors place far greater emphasis on the jockey (the founders of the business) than the horse (the actual business model). While the nature of the business opportunity clearly matters (naturally every jockey needs a good horse, because even the best jockey couldn't do much with an old nag), this is clear confirmation that the people behind the business model – their breadth and depth of experience, their assessed credibility and passion – carry more weight than the business model itself.

A second key theme, and one integral to the point above, is the absolute necessity of a strong sense of vision, passion and purpose. This book will appeal to those 'jockeys' interested in how to take an idea and build a viable and scalable business underpinned by the strong sense of purpose – a clear understanding of the 'why'.

We are also interested in providing insight and encouragement to those in the later stages of their careers who may feel that the runway ahead is limited, including that broad community of intrapreneurs that have real entrepreneurial ambition but are uncertain about how and if they should pursue that. In our view, these realities are amplified in an Australian and New Zealand context by a high degree of embedded ageism in the workforce. We believe with a changed mental model, the depth of experience, networks and judgement of those with long careers presents a great foundation from which to write a new career chapter, and even a whole new career book!

This book is also relevant to investors and policymakers who think about competition and economic growth. We have endeavoured to also embed an educational theme in the book, which may appeal to students in graduate and executive development programs at tertiary institutions – there has been a huge growth in entrepreneurial management and start-up electives at many business schools around the world.

You will also note that we highlight the fundamental role played by physical and mental health. At the very least, starting a new business can be a highly stressful undertaking. Mental health – including, and in particular, resilience – is a hugely underappreciated cornerstone of individual and organisational performance and one of significant interest to both your authors, with one having completed a master's degree in the psychology and neuroscience of mental health at the Institute of Psychiatry, Psychology and Neuroscience, King's College London. We wish we had known more on this topic earlier in our careers. Understanding how the brain works (and sometimes doesn't), how people are shaped by their earlier experiences and environments, and how entrepreneurs should think about coping mechanisms as they manage the stress of uncertainty, complexity and potential failure are fundamental to management and leadership – yet they rarely receive any emphasis in management education.

We apologise at the outset for some of the jargon we use (which we have tried to keep to a minimum). Our story is shaped in the banking industry, so some reference to its inner workings is necessary. Where we have had to use jargon or talk generally about the banking industry, we hope that readers from outside the industry will benefit from the context and insights we provide. Everything we have to say about the banking industry carries encoded principles that are relevant to many other industries.

Also, we wish to make it clear that this is not a book about Judo Bank per se, as it is still a very young company with a big future in front of it.

Finally, before launching into the book, an important disclaimer: the views in this book are solely those of the authors and should not necessarily be interpreted as the views of Judo Bank or of any Judo Bank colleagues past or present.

2

'Project Greengate'

Our entrepreneurial journey begins

Our entrepreneurial journey had its origins in Friday evening beers at the Greengate Hotel in Killara on Sydney's Upper North Shore. As we both lived nearby, we used to meet there to download on the week and discuss issues that were on our minds. We had known each other since our time at ANZ Bank dating back to 2000, and then as colleagues at NAB, where we held high-profile senior executive roles. There was always much to discuss before taking the short walk to our respective homes in time for dinner and the beginning of the weekend.

What is today Judo Bank started life as 'Project Greengate', in recognition of the pub where our early thinking began – and where, to 'close the circle', we celebrated the listing of Judo on the Australian Securities Exchange some six years later on 1 November 2021. A good pub!

Throughout 2011 to 2014, we regularly discussed how the banking industry was industrialising, and how the drive for constant profit growth had resulted in progressively poorer customer experiences. The Australian and New Zealand banking systems had become highly concentrated around the four major banks – ANZ, Commonwealth Bank of Australia (CBA), NAB and Westpac – and their relentless drive to maximise return on equity (RoE) in pursuit of the increasingly short-term targets set by the investment community, while simultaneously being protected from acquisition by the 'four pillars policy'. This had resulted in aggressive cost cutting, centralisation, and a dehumanising and productisation of the industry. We described this process as the 'industrialisation' of the industry.

Despite the poor and progressively declining customer and social outcomes this industrialisation drove, the immense power of the oligopoly continued to underpin strong and ongoing profit growth, making them among the most profitable banks in the world. There was simply no meaningful competition, and the major banks regularly showed little regard for customers, as evident in practices such as increasing lending rates immediately when the central bank increases the official cash rate while dragging their heels in passing on the same increase to depositors, or the classic practice of charging loyal customers a higher interest rate than new customers and relying on customer inertia. It is estimated that the Australian banks make $4.5 billion a year from this customer 'loyalty tax'.

Over time, these trends had engendered a set of industry practices, values and cultures, the products of which became very visible in a public sense through the Hayne Royal Commission in 2018 and 2019 and its subsequent report. The Commission acted as a lightning rod for multiple sectors of society, communicating with a highly aligned view that the banking industry had lost its professional ethos and conducted itself in an unethical manner that was ongoing, and that the chorus of protest was getting progressively louder. The root causes of the problems were crystal clear to us: even though we were in very senior positions inside major banks, our inability to influence direction had been a growing source of frustration in what are highly political, heavily siloed, rigidly bureaucratic and 'path-dependent' organisations, where the 'cultural concrete' was set and defined by a chronic and internally focused bureaucracy.

The banking industry had lost sight of any sense of *purpose* or *social licence*, something we felt passionately about. We always believed that large domestic banks should be there to serve the public interest, balancing this with self-interest goals – an 'and' rather than 'or' philosophy. We felt the industry had fundamentally lost sight of this and had absolutely no understanding of the idea of 'shared value', a concept and area of study pioneered by Michael Porter and Mark Kramer that we subscribed to strongly. We saw this most acutely in the way the banks were engaging with small- to medium-sized enterprises (SMEs), the vast majority of whom felt taken for granted by a powerful industry that was much more interested in pushing mortgages to households and property investors than looking after their more bespoke needs.

Given the oligopolistic structure of the industry, its unique privileges and the uncanny sameness in how the banks operate, SMEs had little practical alternative other than resetting their expectations well down and taking what was on offer. SMEs came to accept the 'triple-U virus' in their relationship with banks: unloved, undervalued and underserved. In practice, this often meant being 'relationship managed' from a faceless call or contact centre, or at best by an overworked banker who had several hundred customers to look after and simply could not look after each one effectively.

Adding to this banker's burden was the perennial uncertainty of being caught up in the frequent reorganisations that have become a very unfortunate part of the natural rhythm of many large banks. These are motivated either by cost cutting or a new senior executive seeking to 'make their mark'. Having been through these cycles numerous times, we both observed the regularity with which those costs were added back in later years when the strategic error of earlier judgement became apparent. This add-back sits alongside the substantial opportunity cost that comes with what are fundamentally inward-facing exercises – more often than not led by management consultants with little practical experience – that drag on the productivity and momentum of the company and, most importantly, the people. In so many cases, these are truly false economies.

The idea of a challenger emerges

We are unashamedly traditionalists when it comes to the banking of SMEs. Our perspective is built on thousands of meetings over time and is founded on the absolute centrality of the relationship with the customer. We believe passionately that SMEs deserve a fundamentally different and better deal than was on offer in the market, given their unique requirements and the critical role that they play in the economy. There are many throughout the banking industry who pontificate on what small business wants without ever having banked an SME customer.

We were concerned that, as the banking industry had developed an unhealthy 'sales' culture, professionalism and expertise – or the 'craft' of SME banking – was being crowded out by a relentless drive to standardise, centralise and cross-sell as many products as could be forced down the throat of SMEs. These trends reflected an industry that chose to 'industrialise' its service proposition for self-interested reasons, not in the name of customer service.

We would regularly reflect on how inward-looking and arrogant the industry had become, and how it was ripe to be challenged by new, hungrier and more agile players. Yet while we saw the emergence of well-funded and successful new players in the much-maligned UK banking sector, there was a deep complacency about the industry in Australia and New Zealand. A stark example of this was the oft-cited belief that superior management and regulation had resulted in Australian banks having avoided the global financial crises that impacted banks and economies in other markets from 2008. This sense of superiority was totally misplaced, as former federal treasurer Peter Costello said:

> 'Our banks are absolutely immune from market discipline, living in a highly profitable cocoon; they think all these high returns are from their own brilliance, but what they haven't understood is they have a unique and privileged regulatory system which has delivered this to them.'

Given the underlying similarities between the UK and Australian–New Zealand markets, the changes that were occurring in the UK banking market did provide a glimmer of insight and hope into what might be possible in Australia and New Zealand if the government and its regulators chose to embrace the promotion of competition in an industry that used its considerable power to lobby against change.

As we thought about Project Greengate, a daunting reality emerged: unlike other industries targeted by start-ups, commercial banking is hugely capital intensive. Our basic initial workings highlighted that, depending on time to full scale, we would need to raise up to $1.5 billion of equity over five years – and many multiples of that in debt – to build a meaningful bank that was capable of being scaled. We could not find a precedent domestically or elsewhere that had achieved such a level of investor support for a new banking business.

From the outset, we felt our proposition was very different from the incumbent banks and the handful of emerging new players in the market. As we built out the plan, we wanted to avoid the 'fintech' and 'neobank' labels – not because there is anything wrong with them, but because they can be lazy categories in which to group what is a broad array of business models. Also, some of these new business models were making exaggerated claims about what they were going to do to the banking industry without being able to point to any credentials to support those claims. Xinja Bank was a classic example of this.

We would regularly cringe when we read media quotes about 'changing banking forever' or 'taking on the major banks'. We saw what was to become Judo Bank as unique, a 'challenger', a 'disruptor' – two words that were new then but are now in relatively common parlance.

We had developed a vision of a relationship-centric SME bank that was a blend of old and new: old in the sense of traditional relationship banking values, and new in the sense of a modern-technology-enabled operating model. In developing our vision, we followed the advice of the author Stephen R Covey from his book *The 7 Habits of Highly Effective People*, which has sold over 25 million copies. One of Covey's enduring pieces of advice is to start with the end in mind. Following that sage advice, we visualised a bank that would become the industry standard for SME banking – not the biggest, but the best. We visualised a bank that could be truly world-class, and we defined the quantitative and qualitative criteria that it would need to meet to be world-class. We also visualised a large bank, not a small niche player, so having a business model that could be profitably scaled was important in how we thought about Project Greengate.

Our advice is that if you think small, this will become self-fulfilling, so always think and plan big. From the outset, we always thought and planned big, despite the occasional askance looks ('You're planning to raise *how much* capital?'). Big thinking is much more attractive to serious investors. It is also attractive to ambitious employees, and serves as a key reference point for the detailed thinking and planning you must do and the nature of the talent you need to have around you to bring your plan to fruition. We had already thought carefully about the calibre and character of people we wanted to work with, and so the aspiration of thinking big was inextricably woven into our talent agenda.

There is a 'but' that comes with thinking and planning big though: you also have to be willing and able to get into the detail early. As one wise counsel told us, given the seniority of our previous roles,

'While your recent backgrounds might have been as generals – at the back of the action, in the tent, scanning the trenches with your binoculars – in young organisations you have to regularly and consciously move between the tent and the frontline trenches'. As we have grown, we have come to think of this as moving from the balcony (the strategic big picture) onto the dance floor (the operational detail), and back and forth. We strongly believed from the beginning that having the dexterity of leadership to move easily between the two is a strong and essential driver of success. We would regularly emphasise to our colleagues that their capacity to do this was a sign of the kind of leadership and management we were looking to build. We all know people who can't get out of the detail to look at the big picture, to understand it and use it as a framing context for the work they are doing. Equally important over time is framing this context for others as they assume leadership positions as the company grows. We all know people who struggle to understand how to move on the dance floor because they've spent much of their lives watching from the balcony.

Having the ability to move between the two perspectives also brings another source of value: being able to consistently provide the context that allows you to bring people with you. In the complexity and detail that characterises the early stages of a company, continuously linking activities, decisions and priorities back to the bigger picture is incredibly important.

Critical advice

Having built our initial hypothesis, we spent a lot of time in London in late 2015 and early 2016, looking at the changing banking landscape and getting to know some of the emerging challengers to the five incumbent 'major banks' there – in particular, the folks at Shawbrook

Bank and Aldermore Bank. Over time, we got to know Shawbrook very well, and we will always be indebted to their then-CEO Steve Pateman and CFO Dylan Minto for the time they gave us. They remain very good friends and almost became shareholders in Judo Bank (more on that in Chapter 6). In our early discussions with Steve at Shawbrook and with Phillip Monks, the CEO at Aldermore, we asked for their two or three key insights on building their businesses since being granted their licences and what advice they would give us. The independent discussions came back with three clear – and what we have subsequently found to be hugely valuable and uncannily accurate – pieces of advice.

First, choose your shareholders very carefully. The right shareholders can add so much value to a business – and have, for us – while the wrong shareholders can consume huge amounts of time, add substantial stress and potentially put the company at risk. It is like choosing a romantic partner: the relationship must have balance – a willingness to give and take – to be able to endure the inevitable stresses and strains over time without folding. Some shareholders can be wrong for your business because they are short-term in nature, looking for profits and dividends at the wrong time for the business, or attempting to frustrate capital-raising efforts or other key initiatives with the aim of protecting their position. This can absorb huge amounts of time and energy, and in so doing work against the interests of the company. It is critically important to avoid the rogue investor who can create much frustration in a business' important formative years. Also, consider the substance of the investors to make sure that they are financially capable of supporting the future capital needs of the business.

We also felt it important that we had shareholders whose reputations and standing in domestic and global markets would reflect well on us; there is an old saying, 'Tell me who your friends are, and I will tell you who you are'. (We know it is easy to say all this when most start-ups are desperate to take money from wherever they can find it. We were fortunate to have a portfolio of good, supportive investors.)

The second piece of advice was that the people who help build the bank may not be the right people to grow the bank, and it is likely that close to 50 per cent of those who start the journey might not be there after three years. That was exactly how it worked out at Judo Bank, as we discuss in Chapters 7 and 8. This is in large part because there is a big difference between building a business and building an organisation. Some people thrive on the chaos of an early-stage business and can become bored with the routine of managing a later-stage business. Some people leave because personal circumstances change, and the demands of a start-up conflict with family commitments. As we discuss later, the fact that people leave is not a reflection of their skills and passion for the business, but more often of what motivates them, and of the evolving needs of a business that is changing apace. How the departure of founders or early pioneers is managed is so important to avoid damaging cherished personal relationships.

The third piece of advice was to be prepared for the real shortage of people able to deal with ambiguity. Everyone will self-nominate as being highly able to do so; however, when placed in the roller-coaster situation of start-ups, the reality is that few are, particularly those steeped in the traditional and rigid routines of the commercial banking industry or any large organisational bureaucracy.

Linked to this advice on people, and particularly on the founding leadership team, is the importance of having people who are abundant thinkers. As Tara Swart wrote:

> 'Abundance correlates with positive thinking and generosity, with the central belief that there's enough out there for everyone… Abundance feeds our self-esteem and confidence and helps us stay resilient during the tough times.'

This is not always a quality found in the commercial banking industry. Abundant thinkers do not allow fear and risk aversion to dominate their thinking.

In addition to our conversations with the UK challenger banks, very early in our thinking we contacted friends in London who had been involved in building and backing challenger banks: in particular, Joe Giannamore and Peter Cartwright, who headed a firm called AnaCap Financial Partners. AnaCap had been the backer of Aldermore Bank, which, together with Shawbrook Bank, had been at the vanguard of the SME challenger bank movement in the UK (both Aldermore and Shawbrook initially specialised in SME banking). We knew Joe through a very good friend, Michael Callen, former Vice Chairman at Citibank in New York. By virtue of the relationship with Mike, Joe and Peter were very welcoming and generous with their time and advice.

A seminal meeting for us was with Joe and Peter at AnaCap in their offices just off Tottenham Court Road in early 2016. Joe is a straight-shooting, no-nonsense Wall Street investment banker. He asked detailed probing questions about the business model, and then said:

> 'Are you sure you want to do this? This will be the hardest thing you guys have ever done or will ever do. Being a big bank CEO is a walk in the park by comparison. There will be many very dark days, when failure is staring you in the eyes – but, if you are successful, you will have more fun than in any other time in your career. It will be an amazing ride, creating something out of nothing.'

He went on to add, as a thudding and sobering reality check, 'You guys are no spring chickens; are you sure you want to do this? There have got to be many better and easier ways to spend the next ten years!' (The younger of us had just turned 50.)

Joe emphasised the message time and time again that this was the hardest thing we would ever do, and it would involve huge personal risk. If we got it wrong, we would both be a lot poorer and have likely exhausted whatever meaningful career runway there was in front of us. The economic concept of opportunity cost took on a real personal meaning. Hard-earned reputations could also go up in smoke, particularly if other people's money was lost. In a close-knit global community, there would be no place to hide. Joe had a sense that the lack of political and regulatory will at the time to allow for new entrants into the Australian and New Zealand banking market added to what was already a high probability of failure. At the end of our meeting, he asked the most important question: 'Why are you doing this?'

Without reflecting on the question (because we had asked ourselves the same question many times at the Greengate Hotel), we ran through our three primary motivators: a deeply held belief that there was a better way to serve the banking needs of the SME economy; a deep passion for the importance of SMEs to the economy; and a desire to build something that would be a legacy, a standard-bearer for how SME banking should and can be done. Personal financial gain was never a driver; we always saw that as a by-product of executing well on what was to us a clear vision: building and managing a well-run bank that was anchored in *purpose*, defined by *values* and crystal clear on strategy. A seminal truth that has become abundantly clear to us over the years is that there is just no way you could sustain the demands of building a meaningful bank, or indeed any business, unless you had that deep passion for it. As Warren Buffett said, 'Making money isn't the backbone of our guiding purpose, it is the by-product of our guiding experience'.

As we discuss in Chapter 8, where there is a deep passion for what you are doing, everything is possible, and you rarely feel like you are working: you are building something and living a life with a clear sense of purpose. Also, as Joe mentioned, there is the thrill and lasting memory of an amazing ride in creating something out of nothing. In a career and personal sense, it can be defining.

So, in essence, began the journey. The candid nature of the advice was worth its weight in gold, and to this day we still reflect on it. During the weeks spent in London, as we reflected over pre-dinner beers at The Flask or The King William IV in Hampstead, we were more than up for this and excited about the journey ahead. We both believed in leading a life of no regrets, and that, even if we failed trying, it would be better than always wondering, 'What if?' During our many visits to London over the years, we favoured Airbnb accommodation, the cost of which was a fraction of that of staying in a modest London hotel. We were also spending our own money, and so every dollar was carefully scrutinised – a behavioural trait that is now deeply ingrained.

During the evenings following our meetings with Joe, Peter and others over a few glasses of wine at dinner, we knew such brave thinking and talk was easy. Wine has the wonderful effect of overwhelming the more rational influences of the brain's executive functioning prefrontal cortex through a dopamine rush (dopamine is one of the brain's key neurotransmitters and plays an important role in the 'reward' neural network and how we feel pleasure). When the prefrontal cortex regained its control the following morning, the reality set in that launching a new bank would be a multi-year journey across fields peppered with landmines and stormy waters full of icebergs (some visible and many not). It was also abundantly clear that it would require a lot of money and, prior to raising our first seed capital in August 2016, that meant co-founder money. As we were to learn, it is very easy to burn through money when you engage consultants, lawyers and accountants, and that is before finding some modest office accommodation to help create team bonding.

Why, what and how

In reaching the decision to push ahead, to begin putting real flesh on the bones of our emerging hypothesis (and despite Joe's sobering warning), we went back to fundamentals. First, why do we want to do this? Second, what is it that we want to do – what form does it take, and what does it look like? Third, how are we going to get this done? This is the classic 'why, what and how' model. No clichés here: these were big, important and very serious questions that, as we answered them and come back to check against them, have always served to reaffirm those early framing ideas and principles.

The first question – *Why?* – was easy, containing two key elements. Firstly, and most importantly, we talked at length about the centrality of *purpose* at both a commercial and personal level. We wanted to build a pure-play bank that was anchored by a strong sense of purpose, which defined and guided everything that it did. Secondly, we felt there was a huge market opportunity: that the banking industry had poorly served the SME economy and, driven by its oligopolistic complacency, had taken SMEs deeply for granted. You only had to scratch the surface to get a sense of the antipathy toward the major banks, who controlled close to 85 per cent of the SME banking market, and from which they extracted high returns. We had both had numerous conversations with international commercial and investment bankers who were utterly astonished by the returns being made by the Australian banks in contrast to their equivalents in other developed markets around the world. This is what economists call a 'market failure': a situation in which the allocation of goods, service or capital by a free market is not what is called 'Pareto efficient', leading to a loss to the economy (in other words, in pursuing their self-interest, banks created outcomes that are not efficient for the economy). We felt there was a big opportunity here if we could build a bank that solved for this problem. Easily said, but far from easy to do!

Analysts and sceptics might sensibly ask, 'If there is such an opportunity, why haven't others sought to enter the market?' This is a good question, which we answer in more depth in Chapter 3 with the three must-haves and the foundational questions, but fundamentally it revolves around multiple high barriers to entry.

The second question – *What?* – was much more complex. The idea of creating a bank was easy in concept, but there was no meaningful history of new banks being created in Australia. The Australian and New Zealand banking market is highly concentrated and, as mentioned, one of the most profitable in the world. There was not much real competition, with the majors being generally focused on delivering to short-term market expectations, maximising RoE, obsessively focusing on 'cost-out' initiatives, and generally avoiding any disruption to what was a very cosy and comfortable arrangement. Also, in 2015, there was no clear pathway to a banking licence. (Changes to the licensing regime did not eventuate until 2018, when the Malcolm Turnbull–led government announced pro-competition reform, modelled to some extent on what had been done in the UK.)

Ironically, equity analysts and investors might have quietly liked this arrangement and not been overly enthusiastic about anything that threatened the status quo. If investors own all the major bank stocks, as is predominantly the case in Australia given the index weighting of the banks, a threat to the economics of the major banks from challengers or disruptors can impact portfolio performance. As fundamentally ex-growth institutions, the major banks are dividend cash cows, which investors understandably like! APRA (the Australian Prudential Regulation Authority), the highly regarded and conservative bank regulator, had a mandate to ensure stability, and there is nothing more stable than the status quo.

Given the uncertainty of getting a banking licence in 2015, we worked through the various alternative vehicles to a banking model, including a non-bank financial institution or a specialist fund manager.

Having approached the question from several angles, we kept returning to the same conclusion: if we wanted to build something capable of scale – and with the ability to attract the volume of capital and funding we felt it would ultimately require at scale – then it had to be a bank. This was despite all the added capital required and the additional administrative and governance costs associated with the privilege of having a banking licence.

Several of our initial prospective investors wanted to talk about funding us into the acquisition of an existing enterprise that came with existing technology, customers, asset base and revenue line, which we could use as a platform to build on and shape toward our espoused vision. This was dismissed early in our thinking. What we did not want was to spend the first three or four years 'rewiring' and dealing with legacy problems, as Aldermore and Shawbrook had done. This comes with the legacy culture that you get in most organisations, legacy technology, legacy infrastructure and assets, legacy data and legacy thinking. We had a very clear vision of what we wanted to build, and that was a new and unique bank, which built from scratch would clearly reflect our vision and approach. Self-evidently, though, this was also profoundly harder and riskier to do; but sometimes it's better taking the long road, because it gets you to the destination you're really looking to travel to.

We also felt that the additional costs of being a bank would be offset by the lower risk premium attached to a firm regulated by one of the world's most respected banking regulators. We felt that many of the people we would want to hire, the SMEs we would want as our customers and the investors we wanted to attract would take comfort from our subjection to close regulatory scrutiny.

Of course, the ability to access the deposit market to fund the bank was another important consideration, but not the primary one. Bank-held deposits in Australia are subject to a taxpayer guarantee of up to $250,000 per individual deposit at an individual bank. This is one of the many reasons banking is such a uniquely privileged industry and the concept of a social licence is so relevant. There are no other private sector industries that are essentially backstopped by the taxpayer; hence banking is in so many ways a quasi-nationalised industry, at least for the major banks.

So, the decision to build our new business as a bank was one that we came to easily in the end, but only after a careful analysis of the pros and cons, as per our mantra 'measure twice, cut once'. Our strong advice is to not rush big decisions: too many new ventures rush critical decisions and live to regret it later.

The third question – *How?* – was challenging in many ways, but easy in others. We strongly believed that while *financial* capital was always going to be critical, more important was *human* capital, so priority number one was to assemble a high-calibre team of like-minded people: people who understood and passionately believed in the SME thesis and would be a good cultural fit for what we wanted to build (we come to what we call 'cultural capital' in Chapter 7). Oh, and we wanted people who were willing to both invest their money in the business and work for nothing until we had raised some serious capital, which is a big ask. Asking the founder team to invest their own money in what was still a PowerPoint concept was both a measure of their commitment and a technique to mitigate the risk of key people leaving when, as would inevitably be the case in the early stages, we hit stormy waters and failure became a higher probability.

In thinking about the people who we would target as the founding employees of the bank, we compiled a list of approximately 75 names, which we narrowed down to eight. We got seven of the eight, which was excellent (and reassuring).

We wanted to build a truly cross-functional team, so we avoided duplication of core skills, although all the key executives we targeted had broad career experience in banking. The key co-founders were Tim Alexander, an experienced banker who had spent his career at

NAB across many roles and understood SME banking from A to Z, and Chris Bayliss, who we also knew from NAB and was then with Standard Chartered Bank running their Personal Banking across Asia. Chris was keen to return to Australia, and we knew him as a multi-talented and first-class executive with extensive experience across many markets and in many roles. Both Chris and Tim's appointments and their pioneering work have been critical to Judo's success. So, too, was that of Kate Keenan, another early member of the founders' team, who had worked closely with us at ANZ and NAB; Kate brought a huge amount of can-do attitude and an entrepreneurial mindset, evident in her skilful negotiation of many aspects of operations, including marketing and brand management.

Several other co-founders were soon to join the team. The first was Alex Twigg, who was with Woolworths but had an extensive start-up background in Australia, the USA and the UK. Alex's core expertise was in technology, and he was very important to what we were building; with a first-class intellect, he was also the only credentialed entrepreneur in the team. An equally important appointment was Mal Hiscock, who had a keen eye for detail and an incredible work ethic, and who we both knew from our time at ANZ. Mal had an extensive corporate finance and investment banking background, which was very valuable to the early formation of the firm, putting in place complex core transactional agreements that were critical to our capital-raising goals. We also targeted Jacqui Colwell, who had extensive banking experience across many roles and deep insight into both the relationship and risk-management aspects of SME banking. Bringing Jacqui in as a co-founder and our first Chief Risk Officer (CRO) was a critical appointment, as was the later appointment of Megan Collins as our Head of People & Culture, who built on the early work of Cécile Scott. As a key part of the early team, we also had Arun Nangia, a highly experienced international banker who was a very effective sounding board on a whole range of issues.

We continued to add to the team, and we were delighted and reassured by the co-founder team's capacity to attract high-calibre individuals such as Frank Versace, George Obeid, Ben Tuszynski, Michael Heath, Darrel Thomas and others. Having said that, assembling a high-calibre team with deep and relevant expertise was one thing; forming a cohesive and high-performance team is something very different. As Patrick Lencioni wrote, 'Building a cohesive leadership team is the first critical step that an organization must take if it is to have the best chance at success'. Many entrepreneurs make the mistake of assuming that building a cohesive and high-performing team will happen naturally, and like management, is a less pressing issue than getting product to market. This is a very big and, sometimes, defining mistake. More on this in Chapter 8.

The 'how' as played out by David and Goliath and *Ted Lasso*

At the beginning, and throughout the evolution of Judo Bank, we often reflected on the parable of David and Goliath as brought to life by Malcolm Gladwell in his excellent book of the same name. To us it captured simply and powerfully the spirit of the industry that we were seeking to compete in and our philosophy on how to compete, bringing a story to life in everyday settings of how the underdogs can and do take on the giants… and succeed.

The first thing to recognise about staid industry giants is that they are not always what they seem on the surface. They are rarely as strong as their dominant presence might suggest: they are often riddled with weaknesses. Understanding your competitors' weaknesses is so important in developing strategy, as we discuss in Chapters 3 and 4. In Goliath's case, his reality was that he was a half-blind, lumbering giant with virtually no agility who had to be led onto the battlefield.

Across so many industries, giants have vision problems and suffer from severe cognitive dissonance: a fundamental irreconcilability of their desire to act with their capacity to do so. For David, the driver of his success was fundamentally to reframe the contest and avoid competing with Goliath on his terms. David's reframing was simple: going to battle with superior technology in the form of a sling. He could compete without getting close to Goliath. Fascinatingly, Gladwell points out that the stone from David's sling that hit Goliath in his only vulnerable point given body armour, his forehead.

So it is in business when your opponent has certain advantages. Never engage in competition on the terms defined by a giant. A close-up battle was never going to favour David, and a distance battle was never going to favour the near-blind Goliath. David was clear on what his competitive advantage was and designed his entire strategy around it, and executed his strategy perfectly. The parallels between the David and Goliath parable and the 'Judo strategy', which we discuss in Chapter 4, are uncanny.

While it is a useful metaphor to illustrate a foundational perspective, there is a point at which we move past the David and Goliath parable. We were not fundamentally in a battle with giants; we were in a battle to define a strategic position and value proposition that would underpin a successful business regardless of what the giants did. In essence, the name of the game was to focus on our own performance, our own standards, and work hard over time at making them not only competitively differentiated but the very best in the market.

The story of Jack Taylor and Enterprise Rent-A-Car really resonated with us. Jack entered the car hire business in 1957 at age 40 (a ripe old age in those days, a spring chicken today!). Enterprise started with 17 cars in an industry dominated by giants such as Avis, National and Hertz, who controlled the critical airport locations. Notwithstanding huge disadvantages relative to the giants, and with only 17 cars, Enterprise grew through great customer service, and several decades later it was worth more in market value terms than all the giants added together. How could a new entrant with only 17 cars survive, let alone succeed, in an industry dominated by giants who have huge advantages such as critical airport locations, and scale and scope economies? Answer: great, truly differentiated customer experience! Enterprise rented the same cars as the giants – there was no product or price differential – but offered a truly differentiated customer service experience. The story of Enterprise had huge parallels with Judo: it was a story that said everything about how we sought to compete and succeed.

In so many ways, Jim Collins captures the emphasis of this in his excellent book *Good to Great*: 'The good-to-great companies understood that doing what you are good at will only make you good; focusing solely on what you can potentially do better than any other organization is the only path to greatness'. In Chapter 3, when we talk about the power of specialisation, this is fundamentally what Collins has in mind.

This was also exemplified in the amusing TV series *Ted Lasso*, in which an American football coach goes to England to coach an English Premier League soccer team despite having no prior understanding of soccer or the culture in England. In one episode, facing relegation, Coach Ted dreams up several plays based on American football and, of course, nearly creates a shock win against all the odds. As both the newest player on the field and the underdog, you must do something fundamentally different and better than anyone else. Doing the same is predictable; you need to find an alternative strategy that forces the business to be creative and innovative.

Nothing drives innovation more than the absence of a natural advantage. Conversely, giants have little real motivation to innovate, as Clayton Christensen highlighted in *The Innovator's Dilemma* (which we explore further in Chapter 4). Giants in most industries compete in the same way as they always have; they've typically prospered in their environment they see change as a threat to their comfortable and dominant position. In banking, this competition is so often around price and risk appetite. These are short-term levers, devoid of any real value-adding, that eventually run out of runway and can often lead to suboptimal outcomes.

Further considerations

Along with our deep interrogation of the 'why, what and how' of Project Greengate, there were several other areas that required focus.

Avoiding drinking too much of one's own Kool-Aid

Over time, particularly if the business is going well, there is the temptation to start believing that because you are good at something, surely you should be good at something else that looks and feels a bit like it. We labelled this 'drinking too much of your own Kool-Aid', or being drawn in by the 'shiny baubles just off the main path'. Of course, this doesn't mean that the business can't or shouldn't grow over time into natural adjacencies, but it is essential that there is a very clear and realistic self-assessment of the congruence and execution of those moves against the core source of competitive advantage.

In a similar vein, one of the many traps new businesses must avoid is confirmation bias: the belief that, because you are new, small and free from legacies, you are therefore agile and innovative. With the right mindset and belief system, being an underdog is a wonderful advantage, but success does not always follow. Never forget the 'mini-me' risk: it is easy for new entrants in traditional, regulated industries to sleepwalk into becoming nothing more than a small version of Goliath. One of the biggest challenges that a disruptor or challenger faces is to stay a 'David'. We discuss the 'mini-me' risk further in Chapter 9.

A winning attitude is also critical. Visualising success is a hallmark of a winning attitude. Great Olympians visualise the event they will compete in numerous times in their minds before the actual event. They visualise their success and believe that they can achieve their goal. When it comes to knowledge and the building of ideas, Einstein put it simply: 'Imagination is more important than knowledge'. This goes for attitude: only accept success, no matter what the giants are doing.

Getting up on the balcony

An important factor behind our early momentum is that we met daily, and spent considerable time over lunch or dinner once a week brainstorming, scenario-planning and reflecting on how we were thinking, and raising concerns we each individually might have. Chris, Kate and Tim also played an important role in our early brainstorming, joined in early 2017 by Frank Versace, George Obeid, Ben Tuszynski, Michael Heath, Darrel Thomas and others.

We have always fundamentally understood the importance of time together away from the hustle and bustle of the dance floor of daily activity, and getting up onto the balcony to make sure things are heading in the right direction and we are not missing anything that could prove defining. We would often reflect on Joe Giannamore's cautious counsel that we were 'no spring chickens' and that, not only was this a very high-risk project, but meaningful career plan B's might be harder to find – not to mention that our depleted finances, built up over many years, might evaporate!

Location

We decided very early on that we would locate the business in Melbourne, even though at that time we both lived in Sydney.

There were several factors behind this decision. First, James Flintoft, whom we knew and respected from our time at ANZ, was a senior official in the Victorian Government's Department of Economic Development, Jobs, Transport and Resources. James had heard about Judo in the market and had his team contact us, encouraging us to base the business in Melbourne. We were hugely impressed by how they passionately sold the virtues of Melbourne over Sydney or elsewhere. Second, our research showed that operating costs in Melbourne were up to 20 per cent lower than in Sydney. Third, because we had both spent much of the previous two decades at Melbourne-based ANZ and NAB, we had a good talent network that we could recruit from. So, putting self-interest aside, we concluded that the best interests of Judo would be served by basing the head office in Melbourne. (The political handling of the COVID-19 pandemic by the authorities in Victoria through 2020 and 2021 subsequently caused us to question the logic of that decision on many occasions.)

Looking forward

As we turned our minds to the more detailed and investor-ready business case for the bank, it became very clear to us that this was going to be a totally consuming, 24/7 endeavour. Resilience, perseverance and hard work were going to be minimum requirements, and accountability and risk would well and truly look us in the face every morning and every evening. There would be no big bank committees to hide in, others to blame, huge reserves or resources to fall back on, or convenient provisions to hide mistakes in. Building a new bank (and indeed any new business) has many facets to it, and careful project and risk management are critical. Doing this with like-minded people you know and trust is so important.

Pleasingly, because we had discussed and thought through this project in detail, we stopped asking ourselves, *Are you sure you want to do this?* Success was going to depend on a deep conviction that we would make this happen. Sometimes in life, *not* having a plan B is a good thing: it forces you to make sure that plan A succeeds. We had a steadfast determination that plan A was going to work.

So, the next challenge was to develop a detailed first draft of a business plan that would get us there. It is so important to know where you are heading and how you will get there, avoiding the trap of the Cheshire cat in *Alice in Wonderland*, who, to paraphrase, said, 'If you don't know where you are going, any road will get you there'. This is a big mistake we have seen far too many start-ups make.

3

Measure twice, cut once

From vision to business case

The first major task for Project Greengate was to build a robust business plan, covering strategy and underpinned by absolute clarity on risk appetite, target market, competitive dynamics, people, operating model, regulatory framework, technology and, of course, the financial and economic model. The more time spent on this, the better, to avoid the costly and often embarrassing need to pivot in the future to a new business paradigm – a move we see too often with start-ups that inevitably impacts investors' confidence.

This is a classic case of 'measure twice, cut once'. The beginning of the journey to building the business is a truly unique time in an organisation's evolution. It needs to be thoughtfully planned. While some errors will inevitably be made, poor judgement, insufficient critical challenge and bad foundational decisions made at the outset – such as poorly researched or thought through assumptions, hiring the wrong people or taking in the wrong shareholders – can be defining. At a minimum, they can be difficult, time consuming and expensive to correct; at worst, they can disable the company's capacity to execute and scale, leading to its ultimate failure. Thiel's Law, named after start-up guru Peter Thiel, hits the nail on the head: 'A start-up messed up at its foundation cannot be fixed'. Fractured foundations can bring the whole business down – if not immediately, then highly probably when under stress. This insight is so important and should never be glossed over.

Purpose, values and core beliefs

As a precursor to beginning the build of the business plan, it was important to step back and define our vision.

Purpose

With Chris, Kate and Tim, we had spent months and years discussing *purpose*, so there was deep alignment. However, it had to be clearly, crisply and authentically spelt out as a foundation stone of our growth from the outset, something that would underpin and anchor everything that the new bank would be. A business can change its strategy over time – and some do this regularly – but purpose should be enduring. It should act as a compass that guides all major decisions, and as a lens or filter through which all strategic options are assessed. It should form the basis of a deeply held view of all those in the company about why we, as a company, exist.

It should also act as an anchor or mooring in difficult times. As Peter Drucker famously observed, 'That business purpose and business mission are so rarely given adequate thought is perhaps the most important cause of business frustration and failure'.

We settled on the following purpose statement:

To Be the Most Trusted SME Business Bank in Australia

There is a nice simplicity and clarity about this. Going back to the Jim Collins quote about doing something fundamentally better than anyone else, the above statement was and is the antithesis of the

Australian banking reality. We saw a banking industry that was devoid of trust, and yet the essence of banking is that of trust. The banking industry was once defined by trust: the word 'credit' comes from the Latin *creditum*, meaning to believe or trust. The banking industry reality is that there had been a growing deficit of trust for more than a decade, and that should not be the case in such a societally pivotal and privileged industry.

Great businesses, such as Apple, are purpose-led. Apple's purpose is to create products that enrich people's daily lives: simple, powerful and trusted. For us, building a pure-play SME-focused bank that was a purpose-driven specialist rather than generalist bank was all about the relationship between banker and customer, where that trust is earned over years through consistency of engagement, depth of understanding and shared experience.

We believe that clarity of purpose when evidenced through one's actions is one of the key determinants of both surviving and succeeding in business. As we outline in the coming chapters, while it's one thing to define one's purpose, it's another again to proactively embed it into the way you operate, and the Judo co-founder team worked hard on doing just that. The clarity of that purpose and congruence with one's observed actions also engenders trust, and we both subscribe to the philosophy that trust 'arrives on the back of a tortoise and departs on the back of a galloping horse'.

Values

To complement the purpose of the company, we considered it very important that from the outset we had clear and authentic *values* that would guide the culture we, the co-founder team, wanted to handcraft. We agreed on four Values: *Trust*, *Teamwork*, *Accountability* and *Performance*. These are simple and powerful if authentically held and, as with purpose, evident in everything that we do. As we talk about in Chapter 7, we are passionate believers in the 'multiplier effect' of a strong progressive culture, so we worked hard to incorporate these values in a practical real-world way as we hired staff and built the operating rhythm of the company. (We cover this in much more detail in Chapter 9.)

Some entrepreneurs may feel that focusing on purpose and values is very much 'top end of town' corporate spin. We understand that criticism. These important artefacts of large businesses have become devalued in the eyes of employees and customers because the promise does not accord with the reality of their lived experience. These purposes and values are most often devised within the uppermost levels of the company and rolled out with much fanfare, with key rings or plastic wallet-sized cards to remind you what the values are in case you forget, and then sit in frames on walls that people walk past dozens of times a day but cannot recall the content of. Oh, and they change about once every five or so years.

That does not mean, however, that being clear on purpose and values is not important to a business, regardless of its size. If entrepreneurs can clearly define these two things and practically wind them into the day-to-day functioning of the business as it grows, they can be very powerful and become central to strategy – and, importantly, culture – as the business grows. They are also critically important if the company wants to scale without devolving into a 'mini-me'. The enduring truth is that businesses that succeed over time have clarity of purpose and values. These remain fixed, while strategies, leadership teams and the business model can adapt to market realities.

Core beliefs

We also held a strong view that great institutions are built on a series of clear core beliefs; and so, as well as crisply defining the organisation's purposes and values, it is also important to define its core underlying beliefs. We felt strongly about this because we had observed that many once-great institutions had lost sight of their core beliefs.

As explained in the previous chapter, in essence the genesis of Judo was the belief that there was a market failure in the provision of credit to the SME economy by the banking system in Australia and New Zealand, which had become heavily biased towards mortgage lending. There are reams of statistical evidence underpinning this statement; it is not a question of opinion, nor is the high level of dissatisfaction that SMEs had with the service they were receiving from a heavily concentrated banking system.

Another of our core beliefs was that, in addressing the information inefficiencies that plague SME banking, human judgement has an important role to play. While technology is a critical enabler of how Judo serves its customers, we are defined by a traditional relationship-bank model, with skilled bankers sitting across the table from the butcher, the baker or the candlestick maker – bankers who take the time to get to know and understand them, and have the delegated authority to make the decisions that affect them.

Clarity on what type of business Judo Bank was to become was so important. As we discuss in Chapter 4, we were building an *experience-based* business, as distinct from a product-based or platform-based business. We believe in the 'craft' of SME Banking, where lending decisions are made on the 4C philosophy of credit risk management:

1. Character (reputation, track record and integrity of the owners)
2. Capacity (cash flow)
3. Capital (the equity already in the business – the owners' 'skin in the game')
4. Collateral (security, such as property).

The Australian and New Zealand banking industry typically defaults to the fourth C, collateral, with 95 per cent of all bank lending decisions predicated on the availability of property as security.

We believe that more competition in SME banking is fundamental to the health and progress of the sector and the owners and employees that work within it, and that new entrants into the banking sector must be able to demonstrate the 'three must-haves':

1. **Access to material levels of capital for the first five years of operation:** At Judo, as the size of the opportunity became clear, the need to raise well over $1 billion of capital also became clear. Too many new players seek to enter the market without investor clarity on future capital needs, and this is a major cause of failure.
2. **A clear and sustainable competitive advantage that meets a market need:** What is the problem we are seeking to solve that incumbents can't or won't? That competitive advantage should be anchored by a strong sense of purpose.
3. **A strong management team:** The management team should have deep domain expertise and a demonstratable senior track record in all aspects of banking. This is not a business for novices.

We believe that a weakness in any one of these areas represents a material risk. (Linked to the third 'must-have' is the power of 'founder centrism' as a core underpinning of a differentiated culture, which we explain further in Chapter 9.)

We also believe that being a bank is a highly privileged accreditation granted by banking regulators on behalf of society. With this privileged position come obligations and responsibilities to conduct business in a manner consistent with the concept of a social licence. Banks are unique institutions, and so it is right that they should have unique expectations placed on them by the society they are there to serve.

We discuss many of these core beliefs elsewhere, but key at the outset was being clear not just on our vision but also on the core beliefs that underpinned our business case. We also found that, having spent the time distilling these beliefs as a discipline for ourselves, being able to succinctly articulate them was a big advantage in subsequent discussions with investors, as one way or other the conversations always came back to these underpinning beliefs.

Business model

As we worked on the business case for Judo in 2015 and 2016, we needed the assistance of a skilled financial modeller, which neither of us, nor the other co-founders, were (or had ambitions to be!). The last time we had done any financial modelling was on an Excel spreadsheet many moons ago. Buying *Financial Modeling in Excel for Dummies* was considered a possibility, but the idea was quickly dismissed: we reassured ourselves that, in an opportunity-cost-of-time sense, there were more productive uses of our skills.

Fortunately, we were able to enlist the help of a good friend, Vimpi Juneja, to work with us on the business case. Vimpi was a Harvard MBA and first-class critical thinker who understood banking, and was known for always providing unvarnished but always constructive opinions. Vimpi suggested that we also speak to David Moloney at the Internal Consulting Group (ICG) for assistance on building the financial model. We knew David from his time at consulting firm Oliver Wyman, and he has a first-class reputation in the banking market.

Our first bill was about to come our way, as David and Richard Dale worked on unpacking UK challenger bank business models, as well as building an early financial and economic model for Project Greengate. They did a good job given the maturity of our thinking, but the evolution of our financial modelling – a cornerstone of our business planning and, ultimately, capital raising – was to become an expensive headache until our co-founder (and then, during a critical period for the company, CFO) Chris Bayliss took control of it, reconstructing the model for the third time. Our engagement with sophisticated investors, particularly the Abu Dhabi Investment Council (ADIC), highlighted how rudimentary our early financial model was in dealing with various modelling assumptions. There were many expensive lessons learnt in this process of getting to a financial model we were satisfied with, as we discuss in more detail in Chapter 6 on winning the hearts and minds of investors, but investing the time and dollars into getting it right was hugely important.

In developing the business case, we had threshold questions that we needed to address at the outset – foundational questions that both prospective investors and high-calibre employees would ask:

- Can we attract investors? How much equity will be needed over the forecast period?
- Can we get a banking licence?
- Can we attract enough high-calibre bankers?
- What is our appetite for risk, and what are the frameworks we will use to manage multiple risks?
- What is our customer origination strategy?
- Can we get the lending and deposit volumes to underpin the business?
- How will we achieve planned margins?
- What will the technology platform look like?
- What is the funding model?
- How will we achieve cost targets?
- How might competitors react?
- How will the business scale?
- What kind of returns could be expected?
- When will the business become profitable?
- What kind of market share can be achieved?
- What are the major trade-off decisions and their costs?
- What are the major risks to success and potential causes of failure?

The answers to all these questions had to be thought through both at the outset and for the multiple years ahead, evolving and improving as the business matured and scaled. We had to have clear and convincing responses based on credible and defendable assumptions. One of the benefits of having both of us doing this was the ability to pressure-test those responses, to make sure they really held water. We would encourage all those planning a start-up to overinvest in this process, to be clear-eyed and comprehensive on what foundational questions investors (and indeed other stakeholders) will use to assess whether there is merit in further investigation. Do not gloss over this important aspect of the business case.

The last question, on risks, we view as critical. You must be well prepared for this, and convincing in words and body language that you are across the prominent risks. In all our discussions with investors, particularly international investors, we were asked, 'What are the top three exogenous risks facing the business?'

Generic start-up risks

For most start-ups, there are five generic risks in the way entrepreneurs think.

1. Overconfidence that you can predict and manage 'tail risk'

'Tail risk' describes so-called 'black swan' events, which come as a surprise and have huge impact but with the benefit of hindsight are often rationalised as predictable. It is a big mistake to come across as playing down major external shocks – don't do it! The right approach is to focus on the consequences and how you would manage them; this paints a picture of both the built-in resilience of the business and the maturity and credibility of those presenting.

2. Arguing that the past is always a good guide for the future

Using the past as a guide for the future is what risk management models in banking do, and this is why banks incur big losses every decade or so. Always keep an open mind to the possibility that the future could be very different to the past, and ask yourself what other scenarios could and should be considered. For example, who at the beginning of 2020 could have predicted that the COVID-19 pandemic would engulf the world for the next three years, the extraordinary liquidity measures taken by governments and central banks around the world, and the follow-on material market meltdown that we saw in 2022 as central banks changed gear on interest-rate policy to combat the resulting inflationary pressures that hadn't been seen for several decades?

3. Not being discerning on the advice you take

Take in information, but be sceptical and highly discerning about whose advice you give credence to. Keep a record of the advice you have received and that which you have chosen to ignore – you'll often find that worthy advice on multiple topics comes from the same source (for example, Joe Giannamore and Peter Cartwright for us).

We know of one start-up that was given strong advice from several sources not to use a particular technology vendor; that advice was ignored, and the business was impacted for years to come. Do extensive due diligence on technology vendors! Technology is often the biggest source of risk for both young and mature businesses. The truth is that, with a small number of exceptions, it is an industry trait of technology vendors to overpromise and underdeliver!

4. Hubris and extravagance

Many start-ups fall into the trap of hubris and extravagance. This can relate to experience, as Liz Wiseman indicates in her excellent book *Multipliers*: 'Experience is not the enemy: it is the hubris that is often the by-product of experience that is our greatest enemy'. It can also come from having access to other people's money. Examples of hubris range from wildly optimistic assumptions about revenue, margin and speed of growth, through to renting expensive office space, prematurely embarking on high-profile marketing campaigns, making outlandish claims and generally getting caught up in the hype that is often a reflection of the overinflated ego of one or two founders.

A classic case of hubris is the story of Greensill Capital, the now-defunct supply chain finance company. The extravagances of Lex Greensill, the founder and CEO of the business, are well documented in Duncan Mavin's excellent book *The Pyramid of Lies*. Such was the hubris of Greensill Capital and their CEO that they were able to convince former UK prime minister David Cameron and former Australian foreign secretary Julie Bishop to become part of the corporate governance apparatus, and thus damage reputations that had been carefully cultivated over many years.

5. Refusing to face reality and not accepting responsibility

Psychologists Carol Tavris and Elliot Aronson wrote an excellent book called *Mistakes Were Made (But Not By Me)* in which they outline the common trait in many driven people or justifying foolish beliefs, bad decisions and hurtful acts. Such people – and we are talking about an awful lot of people – do not acknowledge their own mistakes because they have genuinely persuaded themselves that they did not make them. Former US President Donald Trump aside, we guess that you can think of numerous examples of people you know who fall into this category.

To learn from mistakes, you must first acknowledge them. If you do not learn from them, then there is a good chance you will repeat them. Everyone thinking about a new business model should reflect on what Tavris and Aronson have to say about cognitive dissonance and identify their own blind spots. We come back to the dangers of this in Chapter 5.

On this, the words of George Orwell hold a truth that never fades:

> 'The point is that we are all capable of believing things which we know to be untrue, and then, when we are finally proved wrong, impudently twisting the facts to show that we were right. Intellectually, it is possible to carry on this process for an indefinite time: the only check on it is that sooner or later a false belief bumps up against solid reality, usually on a battlefield.'

The early design principles and vision

Building on our answers to those foundational questions of 'why, what and how', and through the lens of our purpose, values and core beliefs, the co-founder team built out the vision and philosophy for Project Greengate and distilled our early thinking into the following high-level design principles:

- Greengate would be a pure-play bank dedicated to serving SMEs, offering them a true relationship-management service. SME customers would be 'front and centre' for Greengate.
- Specialisation as an SME Bank would be critical to our success. We had long believed that specialisation outperforms being a generalist in all walks of life. This can be illustrated by comparing the times and distances achieved by the decathlon gold medallist at the Olympics to those achieved by specialists in each of the ten sports: on average, across all ten sports the specialist outperforms the generalist by 17 per cent (as shown in Table 3.1).

Table 3.1: The power of specialisation

Event	The specialists	The generalists	Specialist premium
100 m	10.16 sec	10.87 sec	7%
110 m hurdles	13.64 sec	14.34 sec	5%
400 m	41.16 sec	47.82 sec	14%
1500 m	3 min, 42 sec	4 min, 38 sec	20%
Discus	62.76 m	47.17 m	33%
Shot-put	19.86 m	15.18 m	31%
Long jump	8.16 m	7.68 m	6%
High jump	2.24 m	2.04 m	10%
Pole vault	5.33 m	4.69 m	14%
Javelin	83.38 m	64.23 m	30%
Total specialist premium			**17%**

- It would be a national business.
- We would come to market with a simple initial suite of products to meet the majority of SME banking needs and then build on that over time.
- We would carefully craft a detailed employee value proposition (EVP) that attracted highly experienced business banking leaders and executives with deep knowledge of the market and extensive relationship networks. Our purpose, culture and relationship-management model would attract and motivate high-quality people with a pioneering personal risk appetite who were looking for meaning in their careers, and who naturally operated with an 'ownership mindset'.
- In the early years, SME customers would be originated in the majority through an extensive network of specialist brokers and

intermediaries. From the outset, we would treat the broking community as highly valued strategic partners and have them well supported by experienced business banking relationship managers.

- Over time we would expand our organic origination to 50 per cent of all new business, though with the strategic importance of the broker community never being lost.
- Commensurate with building toward becoming a fully licensed bank, we would build industrial-strength risk strategies and frameworks, and detailed appetite statements, driving clear, practical, efficient and useable policies.
- Customers would have direct access to decision-makers, who would spend much of their time managing relationships, not being bogged down in internal bureaucracy.
- 'Easy to do business with' (ETDBW) and 'deeply relationship-centric' would define the customer experience. (The ETDBW theme was very important. We first came across it at ANZ. It is a simple yet powerful mantra, which resonates as strongly today as it did in 2002.)
- Our technology and data would be predominantly cloud-based, with IT as a service that transcends all activities rather than being a standalone specialist function. We saw IT as a critical business enabler of our relationship proposition, rather than a definer, as so many new 'Fintech' players were positioning themselves. We also saw the importance of building a 'data platform' from the outset, which would be critical to our business intelligence (BI) and artificial intelligence (AI) aspirations.
- We would view data as a strategic asset, critical to our BI, risk management and plans for developing AI capabilities.
- Greengate's operations would be streamlined, efficient and uncluttered, with an emphasis on 'one way, same way'.

Policies would be clear and decision-making rigorous, efficient, and quick. Relationship managers would be empowered by an industrial-scale processing and administration system that leveraged the power of technology and data for better, faster and more flexible service.

- Our funding model would start life as very conservative, with excess levels of capital and liquidity, and the usage of basic funding and treasury products. Sophistication in asset and liability management would come at a later stage once the fundamentals were bedded down.
- Greengate would be open to partnership models to expand the range of capabilities and services offered to SME customers.

The business case, including strategic framework and operating model, would be guided and shaped by these principles. We managed expectations internally: it was not necessary to have all these attributes in place from the beginning, but they became a critical part of the vision for what we were building and a yardstick against which to measure progress. While being credible and not too ambitious in our planning, the design work was to be clear on what would make the business competitive and scalable. In other words, what would be the source of its sustainable competitive advantage, and what were the critical success factors? The 'three must-haves' to be successful that we identified earlier overlaid these early design principles.

This is basic strategic thinking taught in any MBA course, and yet it is so often missing in the way that businesses, products and services come to market. Where it is understood, more often the big problem is that it is at a theoretical level but not in an operational sense. That is, how do we make this work? How do we operationalise and execute on this? Over our careers, we had seen many strategic frameworks. One of the best for early-stage planning was introduced to ANZ by Monitor Group (now Monitor Deloitte), a US consulting firm which was headed by the Harvard academic Michael Jensen. The simple framework caused managers to focus and articulate their thinking around three questions:

1. Where to play?
2. How to play?
3. How to win?

In other words: what market segments are you going to compete in, how are you going to compete, and how are you going to succeed? Simple yet powerful, as so many things are!

Having defined the purpose, values and core beliefs, worked through the 'why, what and how' and deduced the series of design principles listed earlier, the co-founder team set about using Monitor Group's framework to identify ten 'headings' or 'chapters' (you could even call them 'pieces of the jigsaw'):

- The Leadership Team/Philosophy
- The Employee Proposition
- The Risk Management Framework/Culture
- The Customer Proposition
- The Product Offering
- The Marketing Proposition
- The Target Market Segments
- The Third Party/Proposition
- The Technology Platform/Philosophy
- The Funding Model
- The Governance Model.

These would make up the first ever draft of our information memorandum (IM).

4

The plan of attack

Competitive advantage and the ability to scale

Throughout the development of the business case, we kept coming back to these questions about our sustainable competitive advantage:

- What is the problem we are trying to solve, and what is the industry context?
- Given that context, where within industry should we choose to play?
- Is our competitive advantage real? Really?
- What are the components that together comprise our competitive advantage?
- Is that competitive advantage scalable?
- What are the pitfalls, and how should we avoid them?

As we discuss in Chapter 7 under 'Learning, unlearning and relearning' and Chapter 8 under 'Hire well to form high-functioning teams', the embedding of this culture of genuine challenge around the core come-to-market proposition – and indeed many aspects of the ongoing running of the business – is one of the most important tools we (and any new business founder) had at our disposal.

Let's examine each of these questions in turn. (The question of pitfalls is deserving of its own chapter, and so will be discussed in Chapter 5.)

What is the problem and industry setting?

Strategic thinking must be framed in a market setting. Too many times in our careers, we have seen strategy work (often consultant-led) that is compelling on a PowerPoint but fundamentally impractical or unimplementable in the real world.

A cornerstone of critically defining our competitive advantage was being clear on what problem we were seeking to solve in coming to market – again harking back to the Jim Collins question of what we were going to be fundamentally better at than the powerful incumbents, and what they were not doing well.

We were also clear that our business model was a domestic one, that we wouldn't drink too much of our own Kool-Aid, and that we would not be distracted by those 'shiny baubles' that are 'just off the path'. So many other start-ups fall into this overconfidence trap. We strongly believe that you must be successful in your own market – the one where all the work and thought brought you to the table in the first place, be that geographic, product or customer – before thinking of others, and always be true to your competitive advantage in entering any new market.

We argued with potential investors who saw our start-up model as too risky that we were not a 0 to 1 start-up but a 1 to n start-up, to use Peter Thiel's framing. In other words, the start-up risk was not as pronounced, because we were a deeply experienced and successful team entering a substantial and existing market where there had been a clear market failure. The market reality was that the domestic banking system had progressively changed, arguably most notably since 2006, and there had been a huge shift to household lending and a de-emphasis on business lending. This trend is detailed in *Breaking the Banks*, a book written by one of the authors.

As banks industrialised their operating model, costs were stripped from frontline customer-facing activity with the creation of centralised operations and call centres. An example of this is this real letter to one SME customer from their longstanding bank (only very slightly edited with appropriate name changes made to protect privacy and embarrassment to the bank):

> Dear George,
>
> We know focusing on your business leaves little time for banking conversation that could help it grow. That is why we've introduced our Small Business Contact Centre: a service team of banking experts with diverse professional experience.
>
> From this month, you will no longer liaise with your current Relationship Manager. Instead, our Small Business Contact Centre is available by phone or email to connect with your business specialist best suited to answer your specific query. You can speak to the same or a different expert each time you call. And because every call is noted in detail, any specialist can pick up right where you left off simply by reviewing past information. All you need to do is call 15 16 17.
>
> This is just one of many new improvements we are making to better support your business needs.
>
> Kind regards,
>
> Big Bank

Of course, this well-crafted but disingenuous letter contains one important message: you no longer have a dedicated relationship banker, and here is the call-centre number. Good Luck! The subtext is that the bank is doing this to cut costs and assumes that the SME will adapt to a new reality of depersonalised service, and life will go on. As all banks are doing pretty much the same, there is little outlier risk.

In large businesses, the endless focus on costs and cost-to-income (CTI) ratio is a product of what Clayton Christensen called 'the innovator's dilemma'. Christensen argued that large firms want to employ their resources in substantial markets that offer higher profits, play to their comparative advantage and allow them to deploy economies of scale and scope. To expect these same firms to meaningfully nurture disruptive technologies and risk significant investment in uncertain outcomes is akin to flapping one's arms with wings strapped to them and hoping to fly. Such expectations, argues Christensen, involve fighting fundamental tendencies in the way big organisations work and how their performance is evaluated. This was certainly our perspective, too. Hence, traditional banks try to acquire fintechs and neobanks to seek some of that 'challenger mindset'.

This is not to say that traditional banks do not spend a lot of money on innovation – they do – but, as discussed in Chapter 7, they also have highly developed immune systems that very effectively seek out and smother the new emerging and challenging activities. Major banks spend billions on innovation each year, but for little benefit. The billions wasted often result in more cost cutting or underinvestment in core capabilities and, therefore, customer service suffers.

In parallel with the fixation on cost-out initiatives, the culture in the industry has become progressively more mercenary, with strong expectations and incentives around products sold and sales completed. Professionalism (including ethical standards) and core skills, particularly in SME banking, have been allowed to fall into a state of disrepair.

As the Royal Commission stated in its findings:

> 'Failings of organisational culture, governance arrangements and remuneration systems lie at the heart of much of the misconduct examined in the commission… In almost every case, the conduct in issue was driven not only by the relevant entity's pursuit of profit but also by individuals' pursuit of gain, whether in the form of remuneration for the individual or profit for the individual's business. Providing a service to customers was relegated to second place.'

To cut a long story short, SME lending became the victim of all these changes, and banks would, in the name of homogenisation and cost minimisation, generally only consider lending to SMEs when there was property offered as security. 'I don't have time to get to know you or your business. Do you have a house? How much is it worth?' These are questions that most small business owners will have heard.

So, to that initial question that frames the competitive advantage we were aiming to base the company on: what was the problem that we were trying to solve? The domestic banking industry lacked any meaningful differentiation or competition, and the result was a market failure in the provision of SME credit. The craft of SME banking had been diminished almost to the point of extinction.

Hence the opportunity for Judo Bank.

Our view then, and now, was that the forces causing this market failure were set in a trend that would not reverse. The industry was on a path-dependent course – a term used to describe a phenomenon whereby history counts, and what happened in the past will determine the future given a resistance to change – and to address the market failure in a meaningful way would not occur if it were left to the incumbents. With close to 85 per cent market share and generating attractive economic rents, they had no real incentive to do anything!

Over and above the paucity of relationship proposition, we estimated this market failure to be in the order of $120 billion of unmet SME credit demand. Macquarie Bank Equity Research estimated it to be in the order of $50 to 70 billion in 2015. We were not assuming that all this unmet demand was credit-worthy, but it still represents a substantial percentage of the total banking system stock of approximately $430 billion of SME loans. (Total banking lending to businesses large and small in 2022 was approximately $800 billion and lending to households, mainly mortgages, was $1.9 trillion, which is approximately the same size as Australia's GDP.) Even if the $120 billion estimate was discounted by 50 per cent, it was a material number. All the evidence that we had looked at reinforced the market failure thesis, and to market observers it also made intuitive sense that, as the major banks became increasingly cookie-cutter in their never-ending cost out initiatives, there were an increasing number of SMEs that just didn't fit those increasingly homogenous and industrialised processes. The data was compelling, including the fact that the stock of SME lending at approximately 22 per cent of GDP in 2022 had been in progressive decline relative to GDP since 2000, and sharply so since 2007.

Where to play?

Clear on the nature of the market failure and, at a macro level, the nature of our competitive advantage, we drilled further into the 'where to play' question. The research guided our strategic focus to areas of the market where information inefficiencies exist and, with them, attractive economics, if the risk management framework is strong. We call this area of the market the 'half-moon' (the term introduced by Judo's Chief Risk Officer, Frank Versace), as shown in Figure 4.1.

Figure 4.1: The 'half-moon'

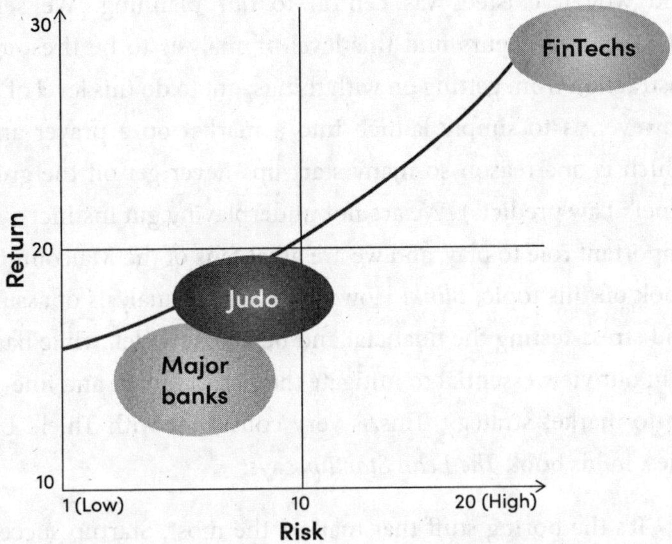

It is the space that the major banks used to operate in before the introduction of Basel II capital risk weighting changes in 2007 and before the industrialisation process took hold and became a dominant feature of the domestic banking sector. It is an area of the market where judgement is applied to an overall business position, rather than an overreliance on algorithms and loan-to-value (LVR) real estate-based measures.

The market failure thesis and low level of satisfaction from SMEs towards the banks was supported by numerous market surveys. This half-moon space was to become our 'blue ocean' strategy (explored in more detail in Chapter 5). We knew that SME customers were hugely dissatisfied with the service they were getting from the major banks, largely due to the progressive industrialisation, productisation and dehumanisation they continued to experience. This dissatisfaction no doubt underpinned the 630 separate SME submissions made to the Royal Commission.

Understanding the size of this blue ocean market opportunity and why it existed was central to our planning. We sense that many entrepreneurs find this level of analysis to be tiresome and a distraction from getting on with things; not to do this level of analysis, however, is to simply launch into a market on a prayer and hope, which is one reason so many start-ups never get off the ground (as Thiel's Law predicts). We are not underplaying gut instinct – it has an important role to play, and we are great fans of the Malcolm Gladwell book on this topic, *Blink*. However, rigorous analysis of assumptions and stress-testing the financial and business model, while hard work, is in our view essential to mitigate the risk of failure and fine-tune the go-to-market strategy. This is very consistent with Thiel's Law. Eric Ries, in his book *The Lean Startup*, says:

> 'It's the boring stuff that matters the most. Startup success is not a consequence of good genes or being in the right place at the right time. Startup success can be engineered by following the right process, which means it can be learned, which means it can be taught.'

Is our competitive advantage real?

It is just too easy to convince yourself that you are something that you are not, to dismiss the hard or penetrating questions that need to be asked, preferring to just 'wing it', to take the risk.

And yes, sometimes this works. Risk-taking resulting in lucky gains activates the same reward circuitry in the brain as cocaine and alcohol, and thus can result in a potentially destructive feedback loop. This is seen classically in gambling addicts. Entrepreneurialism can have a similarly addictive effect on some people who, when hit with a huge dopamine rush, can find that their judgement is distorted, and are convinced of their ability to 'just do it'. This is one of the reasons why all good entrepreneurs should have highly capable people close to them to ensure the risk of impulse decisions is mitigated. Eventually, you will get found out.

We were very determined to not fall into the trap that many in the fintech and neobank communities were falling into: building an app and praying a business model would follow in product markets where the underlying problems they were seeking to solve were not clear – for example, did Australia or New Zealand really need another mortgage lender?

Steve Blank – who has written extensively on start-ups and entrepreneurship, as well as lecturing at Stanford University, the University of California, Berkeley, Columbia University and others – said it well: '"Build and they will come" is not a strategy, it's a prayer'.

Simply wanting to be a technology-led company does not make you one. Too many fintechs define their business by technology and are more 'techfins' than fintechs.

Neobanks and fintechs offer real potential and the possibility of genuine competition to incumbents over time, but there is also the risk of that potential sometimes becoming exaggerated. We viewed technology, including AI, as a critical enabler of success and not a definer of it. We believed from the outset that technology should not be viewed as a classic business function, but that it is core to the entire business operation right across the value chain.

Competition and success in banking depend on more than cheap and easily replicated technology. To offset their funding cost disadvantage and avoid adverse selection, new entrants need a product or a service edge, whether based on deep segment knowledge or specific product expertise. The principle of viewing technology as the core underpinning of an operation rather than a sole source of competitive advantage applies, in our view, far more broadly than to just financial services.

What are the components of our competitive advantage?

Competitive advantage, if it is to be sustainable, is rarely just a question of a technology advantage that others can replicate. Rather, it is a carefully crafted Venn diagram of factors that combine to make a business unique. Competitive advantage must focus attention on those capabilities that lie at the centre of competitive success, rather than at the periphery.

As we set about articulating it for Greengate in that first IM, and in the years that followed as we spoke to investors around the world (who pressed into this from every angle), we saw it very much as shown in Figure 4.2.

Figure 4.2: Project Greengate's competitive advantage

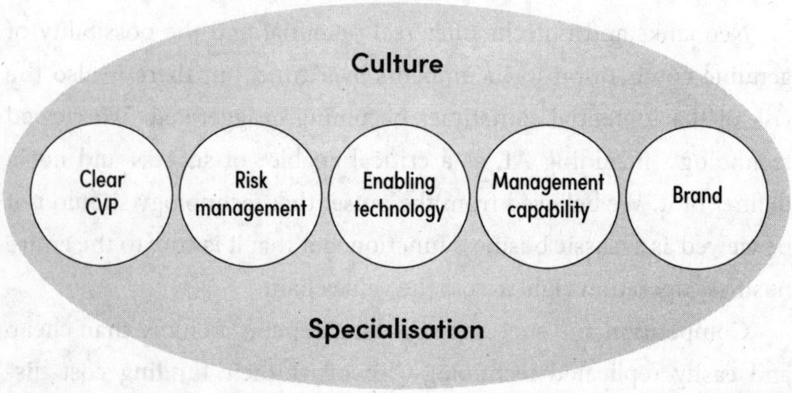

For us a core underpinning of our competitive advantage was that of specialisation. In most walks of life, specialists outperform generalists. People pay more to see a specialist for a reason. As illustrated earlier, in the Olympics, the gold-medal specialists in each sport will outperform the decathlon gold medallist across all categories.

While specialisation is a source of competitive advantage, our thinking on the nature of that advantage was deepened when Lisa Frazier joined our executive team. Lisa has an impressive background across a range of industries, including banking at Wells Fargo in the US and CBA domestically. She had also been a partner at the consulting firm McKinsey & Company in New York. Lisa encouraged us to categorise our business as one of three business models: are we a product-led business, are we a platform provider or are we an experience-based business model? While a business can feature more than one of these models – and many do – there must be a dominant element if a business is to drive superior outcomes. For Judo, that was *experience*. We were to be a relationship-centric bank, and therefore the basis of our sustainable competitive advantage was going to be our ability to provide a superior customer experience – simple, yet powerful. Enterprise Rent-A-Car understood this deeply: their cars were no different from others in the market, just as Judo's loan product is not much different from that of other banks. The quality of the relationship experience, underpinned by being a pure-play specialist, was going to define Judo's strategy and success.

In purpose-building our pure-play specialist and customer-centric business model, we had the enormous benefit of starting with a blank sheet of paper, absent of the burden (and often dead-weight cost) of legacy technology, legacy policies and procedures, legacy complexity and legacy cultures. From day one, the build also reflected the agile nature of our business model and the emphasis we place on being customer-centric, with a target of having close to 70 per cent of our people being in customer-facing (or 'customer-touching') roles, compared to less than 30 per cent inside larger institutions. This is no easy feat in a regulated entity where bureaucracy is encouraged. Jeff Immelt mentions in his book *Hot Seat* that, when GE Capital became subject to US banking regulatory oversight as if it were a bank, it had to employ 5000 full-time employees dedicated to dealing with the demands of the regulatory regime at a cost of nearly US$1 billion per annum.

We also knew that we were *not* building a new bank with the intent to sell it to a larger bank; we wanted to build something that was unique, attractive, sustainable and a legacy. This is an important reflection point for any entrepreneur looking to start a business. We hear many talking about 'exit' and becoming rich by selling out to a larger business. There's nothing wrong with that motivation, but it does bring a very different psychological perspective to decision-making and long-term planning.

Customer value proposition

A clear customer value proposition (CVP) is of fundamental importance. To survive, let alone succeed, a start-up must bring to the market a materially different proposition to what is already in the market. Integral to a sustainable competitive advantage is a crystal-clear proposition on what the business will do and why it is going to be more attractive to customers. What value is the business bringing to market that is currently missing? What problem is the business going to solve that incumbents are not already solving? These are big and important questions. Even if the new business solves a market problem – in our case, the poor service that businesses were experiencing in dealing with banks – how confident can you be that customers will switch? Also, if the business resonates with customers, what do you do if the incumbents look to match the proposition that the new business brings to the market?

Being clear on the differentiation that the new player offers can be the difference between life and death for the start-up. Being clear also on how any competitive advantage can be sustained is critical. What are the barriers to entry and replication? Does the start-up have proprietary assets or unique business model characteristics that others can't replicate?

Risk management

A significant differentiator for us was the speed of our time to decision for both customer and broker. As we see it, the close working relationship between bankers and risk executives in a culture where risk is respected and never compromised is the backbone of delivering on that promise. It also reflects our emphasis on risk management and our cultural goal of an organisation where everyone thinks like a risk manager, within what the industry calls its 'three lines of defence' model. Banking is fundamentally the business of managing risks, and so it is critical that everyone sees themselves as a risk manager. We would advocate this philosophy for most business models: having a culture where people are looking for risks, thinking two steps ahead and asking, 'What could go wrong?' Being paranoid about risk management is not a bad personal trait in an executive, particularly a bank executive.

Technology

Decisions on technology can be defining. As described earlier, we saw technology as critical to our success but as an *enabler*, not a *definer*. This is an important distinction. One of our foundation directors described our business model and operating philosophy as 'high touch, high tech'. This was a perfect strapline that captured the essence of what we were seeking to build. There were too many examples of entrepreneurs falling in love with technology without rigorously thinking through how a sustainable business model could evolve: the proverbial hammer looking for a nail.

In banking, efficient technology can make all the difference to customer service and employee engagement. It can also define growth, scale and profitability. We chose to look at technology as a service and become a cloud-based bank, so we wouldn't own any servers or any technology infrastructure. There are pros and cons in this decision (as shown in Table 4.1), so it is vital that careful consideration is given to whatever decision is made. Don't rush this, and don't immediately go with whatever option looks the easiest or most inexpensive: this can truly be a false economy.

Table 4.1: The benefits and risks of in-house versus external technology

	In-house build and own	Buy and license externally
Benefits	Control over key assets Custom build Proprietary asset	Lower capital expenditure Access to expertise and R&D capabilities Access upgrades
Risks	Complexity Potential not to age well versus new tech High capital expenditure Skilled resources Lower expertise/depth of knowledge internally	Less control Reliability of service provider Speed to market (third parties can be slower than in-house)

Management capability and philosophy

Management capabilities define business success. (Remember the 'jockey' versus the 'horse' from Chapter 1?) As mentioned earlier, we have long held the view that, in the main, businesses do not fail – it is management that fails. Building new, scalable financial services businesses requires experienced and stable management teams – experience, and the judgement that flows from it, is vital. As former Citibank CEO Vikram Pandit said, 'If you're in the credit card business I want to see people who understand how the business works. It's not only about the technology… there is a lot of comfort from seeing the right kind of people in management'. Vikram has invested over US$500 million in fintechs through his venture Orogen.

Too often the public portrayal of fintech executives is that of 'cool', millennial-style entrepreneurs who boast 50,000 to 100,000 customers on their platforms. The residual questions are: Do they have management capabilities to build scalable businesses? Will their 'signed-up' customers make any money? What is the sustainable competitive advantage? As we go on to talk about in Chapter 7, we have spent more time on thinking about our initial and subsequent leadership teams – their capability, breadth of experience and congruence of philosophy – than on any other part of the business.

Culture

Weaving all this together is what we view as our challenger culture: the migrant or feisty underdog and founder mindset that we discuss throughout the book, and the determination and passion to build a truly unique pure-play bank dedicated to the SME economy while avoiding the trap of becoming simply a 'mini-me' version of the large incumbent banks. This is a real trap, particularly in a regulated industry: without vigilant management, it would be so easy to sleepwalk into becoming a 'mini-me', and then your whole *raison d'être* evaporates.

Brand

Brand development was seen as critical, though building the brand that we wanted was very much more a marathon than a sprint.

We made great progress in developing the 'Judo' brand, which was, as with so much else, built on a shoestring budget. The brand had to complement the purpose of the organisation, and it had to be enduring. An indication of just how successful our brand was becoming came when LinkedIn named us Australia's number-one start-up in 2019.

Can we scale?

A critically important early design principle is to build the foundations so that the business is capable of scaling. There are many challenges in scaling a start-up, which we discuss throughout this book. The mechanics of executing on scaling should never be underestimated or left too late in the planning for how the business will evolve.

One such challenge is the hiring of senior executives who were not part of the original founder team. These appointments can be critical to how the business scales and deals with the complexity of growth. There is also the need to bring formal organisation structures and role specialisation into a business where everyone had previously been a 'jack-of-all-trades', and no role descriptions or formal structure existed. This must be done with great skill and care. In the early stages, everyone must roll their sleeves up and do what must be done. People have to be adaptable and agile, which for some is easier said than done. Chris Bayliss, for example, went from being Head of Relationship Management to CFO to Head of Operations and Technology to CFO and back to Head of Relationship Management, all within three years. Tim Alexander also adopted several roles based on business needs. Both Tim and Chris are role-model enterprise leaders.

Culturally, as we discuss in Chapter 8, it is so important to anticipate how the artefacts of scaling can seem to some as a drifting away from the soul and unique attributes of a start-up to becoming a 'mini-me'. They reflect fondly on the early days when adrenaline was high and every day brought its own form of chaos! Managing how new executives are integrated into the business while minimising the negative consequences of the 'old guard' feeling that the business is losing its 'specialness' is critical for managing the growing pains of a young growth company. It is inevitable that some of the early staff – the 'old guard' – will not adapt to these changes and will leave.

We return to these and other challenges of scaling throughout the book, because it is often the biggest risk that a start-up faces once it has navigated the early stages.

5

Dodging blows

Pitfalls to avoid

This chapter covers the following pitfalls that we had to acknowledge and plan to avoid in the development of the business case for Judo Bank:

- Cognitive dissonance
- Bureaucracy
- Uncertainty
- What to call the new bank.

Cognitive dissonance and hyperbole

It is important to avoid hyperbole around overtaking larger incumbents or changing the nature of the industry. Too many new entrants exaggerate their potential without offering any evidence of management competencies to execute on what is claimed. This is a big mistake. In business, humility is a virtue. Let your actions and performance do the talking, not your ego and – a trait we saw occasionally – an addiction to publicity. If there is no substance to claims made, that reality will become apparent sooner or later, and reputations will be weakened if not destroyed. Yet, this is a trap that many fall into. As we mentioned earlier, this problem is endemic. When people are convinced that they have a viable business idea but the market is sending them signals that it is not convinced, they look for information that reinforces their belief and thus do not face a reality that is obvious to others. As the writer James Baldwin – who Johann Hari describes in his book *Stolen Focus* as the greatest writer of the 20th century – said: 'Not everything that is faced can be changed, but nothing can be changed until it is faced'.

People coping with cognitive dissonance will screen out information not consistent with their beliefs. Dissonance theory is a theory of blind spots, and these are dangerous, because they can cause you to make rash decisions or announcements to address the uncomfortable and sometimes stressful feeling of dissonance, which could be damaging in the future. When Xinja announced it had an agreement from a Dubai-based investment firm called World Investments to invest $433 million over 24 months, with the first $160 million to be invested 'immediately', there was much criticism of the premature nature of the announcement when the money failed to materialise, ultimately resulting in the winding down of Xinja as a bank.

Entrepreneurs seeking to demonstrate progress, and who are passionate about their new venture, are highly susceptible to this risk. To avoid this risk, as mentioned earlier, it is important that the senior team has a few trusted naysayers: people who will intelligently challenge and counsel the leader. As we talked about in the coming to market proposition, it is vital that the culture of an organisation promotes challenging and occasionally disagreeing with a dominant leader, and that the senior team has people in it who are willing to enact this, to ensure that the business is not exposed to the blind spot of the leader in the way that Xinja arguably was.

Bureaucracy: the enemy of entrepreneurship

While our co-founder team knew what we wanted as we built out that first IM, we also knew what we didn't want: a core and overriding design principle of our business model and cultural design challenge was the avoidance of the creeping and 'cancerous' bureaucracy that you see inside so many larger organisations. Of course, any bank or business has a level of bureaucracy, but we liken it to cholesterol: some good cholesterol is positive and essential for you. The key is to minimise the amount of bad cholesterol, which clogs up arteries; likewise, damaging bureaucracy is bad for business, because it can stifle innovation, agility and the ability to differentiate.

Too many large businesses are plagued with bad bureaucracy – non-value-added, wading through the treacle of often mind-numbing 'stuff' that grows like weeds all over the place. It becomes an internal industry, which is so evident when you look at the proliferation of job functions, titles and layers of management inside large organisations, the vast majority of which are remote from the customer. As you look across the banking industry, the bureaucracy – and the substantial cost burden that comes with it – has been allowed to develop and remain, protected by the huge economic returns afforded by Australia's banking oligopoly. The level of bureaucracy inside the banking industry would make many public sector departments blush.

An excellent case study into a systemic big company problem with bureaucracy is outlined in Jeff Immelt's excellent book *Hot Seat*, covering his time as CEO of General Electric (GE). Immelt highlighted how bureaucracy had grown inside GE in a way that was slowing down decision-making, suffocating innovation and demoralising employees. He cited work by the Boston Consulting Group (BCG) showing that, while the world had become more complex through regulation, technology, globalisation and faster information (to name just a few forces), organisations had responded with more bureaucracy.

The BCG team had estimated that the world had become six times more complex since 1955, while organisational complexity had grown by a factor of 35. The reality is that too often the paradox of growth is more complexity and bureaucracy, which ultimately kills growth.

You may relate to the reality that so often, any time there is a problem inside a business, another layer of bureaucracy is born; and, as Immelt comments, once it exists, it is very difficult to remove. The governance structure inside many businesses takes comfort in another committee, another layer and another set of checks and balances without standing back and focusing on the core issue. In many ways, governance bureaucracy, which grows like wild weeds, has taken over management accountability and entrepreneurial dynamism in many firms. We return to this important theme in Chapter 9 when we talk about 'founder centrism' and the battle against bureaucracy.

In fact, we come back to the theme of bureaucracy throughout this book, because it is a cancer. At this stage, we give the last word to Gary Hamel and Michelle Zanini from their excellent book *Humanocracy*:

> 'Instead of building human-shaped organisations, we're still hammering out bureaucracy-shaped human beings. If we're complicit in this and have resigned ourselves to the endemic inadequacies of our organisations, it's because we've failed to do our sums.'

Dealing with uncertainty

There is a qualifier to the rigorous planning philosophy we have espoused thus far, which is that an overemphasis on financial plans simply does not work in some start-ups, particularly 0 to 1 start-ups. In a market for something new, while the rigour in the underpinning work is important, how can you possibly be held to a forecast, beyond a well-reasoned estimate with clearly stated assumptions not just about the financials but also about the all-important domestic and global economy? Who in 2015 would have forecast Donald Trump as US President, let alone COVID-19 in 2020? As the great economist John Kenneth Galbraith once quipped, 'the only function of economic forecasting is to make astrology look respectable'.

Equally, even in a market like banking with a 1 to n start-up, how can you be 100 per cent confident in answering the core foundation questions that we listed earlier? Start-ups operate in a world of extreme uncertainty and, by the way, traditional bankers hate uncertainty, as per that very important piece of advice given to us early on about the difficulty many have in dealing with real-world ambiguity. The role of a plan in a start-up is best summarised by the quip from former US President Dwight Eisenhower that 'plans are useless, but planning is indispensable'.

We remember early discussions with Judo's board members in which they grilled us on variances to plans, just as you would inside a stable business model of operating history, industry structure predictability and the comfort of stable environments. In a world of unprecedented uncertainty – the world we live in – planning is a precarious discipline, yet so much of the investor capital market and conventional governance schemata are about 'meeting plans'. The reality is that the first two years of any start-up are years of experimenting and fine-tuning, but hopefully not pivoting (a term we can be highly suspicious of, as it is often used *not* to denote a nudge in a different direction but a significant strategic repositioning). It can be, as Deng Xiaoping said of his strategy for the opening of China in the 1970s, 'like crossing a river by feeling the stones'. This is much more the case in a 0 to 1 start-up but also applies to 1 to n start-ups.

Regarding our economic model, which was going to be subject to much scrutiny by prospective investors, we were confident that, despite the initial absence of scale benefits, it was possible for a small pure-play specialist bank to generate best-in-market returns, based on our experience and a series of clear and well critiqued assumptions. The key is the ability to grow the franchise, so we always saw a nationwide presence as important, starting first in Melbourne and gradually, in a measured way, expanding to Sydney, Brisbane, Perth, Adelaide, Canberra, Hobart and other key business hubs across the country.

We also saw it as important that we could clearly demonstrate the financial and market positioning benefits of specialisation by excelling at SME banking. Playing to your strengths and strengthening your strengths is ageless advice in all walks of life, including sport, higher education, entertainment and business, yet many large organisations lose sight of this. We remember a great address given by then Macquarie Bank CEO Allan Moss to a group of senior executives at ANZ Bank in 2004, when John McFarlane was the ANZ CEO, in which he told the audience that a mistake he often saw in commercial banks was that of overinvesting in weaknesses and consequently underinvesting in strengths. We had seen this when one bank pushed to move its fourth-rated retail division (from four major banks) to third, putting its market-leading business bank division at risk through underinvestment. Moving one business from fourth to third and weakening your market-leading business, potentially causing a number-one business to slip to number two in the market, is not a great outcome, but it is a trap that many large organisations fall into. Our pure-play specialisation model would prevent that problem from ever arising.

In developing the financial model, we also wanted to avoid the trap of underinvesting in operating expenditure during the growth phase of the company. Cost-to-income (CTI) ratios would not be a key focus in the early years. We had seen an unhealthy fixation on the 'Jaws' ratio inside major banks, which is the difference between the percentage of revenue and expense growth. This fixation only ever ultimately served to weaken revenue growth, thus creating the vicious cycle which led to expense cuts and then to further revenue weakness. The reason we describe it as unhealthy is that the analysis of the type and nature of costs was fundamentally lacking. Because of the rigid and often self-protecting nature of bureaucratic costs inside large organisations, there was almost always an underinvestment in the kind of productive costs that drove revenue growth, with the predictable drive towards centralisation and call or contact centres further weakening revenue in later years. Consequently, the culture within banks was not too far away from how Sir Humphrey Appleby puts it in *Yes, Prime Minister*: 'The Foreign Office isn't there to do things, it's there to explain why things can't be done'.

This is just one of the reasons why we are highly sensitive to the nature of bureaucracy – bad bureaucracy, that is – and why in designing Judo, our aim was to have 70 per cent of our operating costs in 'customer-touching' roles and activities, compared to our estimate of less than 30 per cent inside major banks. We also believed that customer-centric, high-performance banks (and indeed other kinds of businesses) should have 70 per cent of their costs in employee salaries and benefits rather than premises and other fixed assets. The crude CTI measure misses so many rich insights and very often leads to poor decision-making. A focus on the nature of costs and a bias towards customer-touching costs should lead to superior economics, and the CTI will look after itself as a by-product of high performance. A high-performance business should have higher per capita costs, because it is paying its people well given the success of the business. It can achieve this while also having best-in-market CTI, which is a goal we had set for Judo Bank.

What to call the new bank?

One big issue for us was what to call the new bank. By early 2016, we felt that the moniker 'Project Greengate' had served its purpose and was now wearing thin; we needed a name to bring the exciting new venture to life. We started this naming exercise by mapping out the key words that came out of our business model and strategic thinking work. Those words included 'SME relationship banking', 'true relationship management', 'customer solution focused', 'agile', 'passionate' and 'easy to do business with'. We also focused on the word 'and', because it served to highlight the balancing of multiple stakeholders, as in 'customer value' *and* 'employee value' *and* 'community value' *and* 'shareholder value'. There were several suggestions, including an early favourite, 'Australian Business Capital Solutions (ABCS)', which had people falling asleep by the time we'd finished the acronym. Fortunately, more creative minds prevailed, and through the excellent work of Kate Keenan we ended up with 'Judo Capital', which then became 'Judo Bank'.

The origin of the name 'Judo' was the review of our initial business case – which was now in the form of an IM – by Vimpi Juneja. True to his analytical prowess, after his review he declared, 'This is a classic Judo strategy!' We quickly googled 'Judo strategy' and found extensive literature, including the seminal work by David Yoffie and Mary Kwak. A judo strategy, in short, is an approach to the generation of competitive advantage that emphasises skill rather than size or strength. It explains why some start-ups or smaller business succeed in defeating bigger, stronger rivals, while others fail. The core strategic problem is, how do you compete with opponents who have size, strength, networks and history on their side? The key insight of the Judo strategy is very reminiscent of Malcolm Gladwell's rendition of the 'David and Goliath' story and how David leveraged his competitive advantage: in entering a market dominated by giants, successful challengers compete in a way that prevents the incumbents from bringing their full strength into play. Judo strategists avoid forms of competition that naturally favour the large and strong, such as head-to-head struggles. Instead, they rely on speed, agility and creative thinking to craft strategies that make it difficult for powerful rivals to compete. There are seven principles of a judo strategy:

1. Operate under the radar.
2. Move rapidly to uncontested ground to avoid head-to-head conflict.
3. Be agile and give way when attacked directly by superior force.
4. Exploit leverage that uses the weight and strategy of opponents against them.
5. Identify your opponent's soft underbelly.
6. Follow through fast; never fall into the role of the defender.
7. Avoid tit-for-tat; think differently.

The legendary business guru Peter Drucker called this 'entrepreneurial Judo'.

'Judo Bank' was a perfect name – one that connected with our strategy and captured our core proposition. Our whole business model was framed with judo strategy–thinking very much in mind. We had a judo strategy, and we fell in love with the name because it came to life as a product of our strategy. We started asking, what it will take to become a black belt? We were able to trademark-register the name without any challenge. The closest we came to a reaction to the use of the name was in the form of a letter to the editor of one of the major newspapers asking why the new bank did not call itself 'Cricket Bank' or 'Wrestling Bank', which was signed by a member of a 1980s Australian Olympic Judo team.

The challenge quickly became that of learning the tools and techniques of how to execute a judo strategy, which became (and continues to be) a big focus of how we have enacted our strategy. Training in the craft of judo strategy remains central to how we compete and how we have grown; it is central to avoiding the fatal 'mini-me' trap. Getting to black belt would be a multi-year journey:

we had to start with a white belt, then yellow, then orange and so on, and keep working hard at it!

A core principle of the judo strategy is to focus on uncontested ground. For us, this meant moving back into the space that banks used to operate in before they became industrialised. In many ways, our approach was a 'blue ocean' strategy, popularised by INSEAD professors W Chan Kim and Renée Mauborgne in their classic book of the same name. A blue ocean strategy essentially is to occupy a space in the market that is not occupied by tired competitors in head-to-head competition with little to differentiate them. The metaphor of the blue ocean represents an uncontested market, in contrast to 'red ocean' – a marketplace where fierce competition stains the water with the 'blood' of the incumbents.

*

Very mindful of Thiel's Law, the co-founder team spent six very intense months on the process of building the business case and financial model. It was probably the most important time of the whole journey. By mid-2016, we were ready to get moving.

We had 'measured twice and cut once'. We had comprehensively worked through the 'why, what and how', distilled the key business principles from that, built those principles into a series of practical 'chapter headings' that had begun to detail the execution framework, and critically stress-tested the nature of our competitive advantage. We were convinced our credentials would stand up to the close (and sceptical) scrutiny that was about to begin. We were more than ready to take the master's degree oral dissertation exam, feeling confident of passing with distinction.

The reality, however, is that this was only the start!

6

Hearts, minds and money

Securing investors

Now that we had a well-developed business plan and the first of the five IMs that we were to draft over the coming years, we needed to enlist the support of several professional service firms before we were ready to get in front of potential investors. Having advisors lined up adds hugely to the credibility of the proposition when engaging with investors. The problem was that our own financial resources were not boundless, so careful negotiation was essential.

Good legal advice is an important place to start. On the recommendation of a former colleague, Kate Olgers, we approached Jonathan Gordon and Stuart Dullard at Ashurst in Sydney and explained what we were looking to do. They quickly understood the concept, our pre–capital raising position and the financial constraints that we were under. To their eternal credit, they backed us, and so began one of the most important relationships in Judo Bank's story. Similar discussions were held with the PR and corporate affairs firm Cannings Communications (introduced to us via whiteGREY, part of WPP, who had helped us build the Judo brand), where we met with Renée Bertuch, Luis Garcia and William Roberts. Again, so was formed one of the bank's early valuable relationships. We also spoke to accounting and advisory firm Pitcher Partners in Melbourne, largely on the back of an existing relationship that we had with Alison Wood from their Sydney firm. Pitcher Partners provided us with much critical support across a range of functions in our formative years and were great to work with. We also needed help with a more detailed financial model, and so we approached Mal Hiscock at boutique corporate advisory firm Orion Corporate Advisory Services. We knew Mal from ANZ Bank, where he had once headed the Mergers and Acquisitions practice. Mal and his business partner, Robert Shorten, agreed to provide corporate advisory services, but largely financial modelling advice, contingent on a successful seed capital raise. Orion supported us through our first seed capital raise in late 2016, and Mal became a co-founder of Judo shortly thereafter, performing the roles of CFO, Company Secretary and eventually Chief Capital Management Officer.

One important piece of advice that we would offer to all those in the foundational stages of business building is to spend a lot of time on the financial model, and to carefully document how the model is constructed and how it works, making sure that all assumptions are clearly stated and explained. This is both for the internal building of familiarity with the model itself and its ease of use, and for those early-stage investors who want to understand the model and its assumptions so they can sensitise individual elements as they do their due diligence. We did not do this well at the outset, and we had to rebuild the model several times and at great cost. Financial models for a bank are, by nature, very complex, but solid and robust financial modelling of the business plan is critical when attracting investors, and this requires lots of effort and lead time. We underestimated this and, as a consequence, we probably spent half a million dollars on the model and associated work over its many iterations. If we had been more careful and thoughtful at the beginning, we could have avoided 80 per cent of that cost. Measure twice, cut once!

We were close to a year into the process and had been funding everything with our dwindling personal resources. A major development was our good fortune in convincing Chris Bayliss, Kate Keenan and Tim Alexander to join us full-time without pay. It was a huge personal commitment and vote of confidence in their belief that we could pull this off. Chris, Tim and Kate were pivotal in our formative period – true co-founders.

Seed capital

With many of the important pieces of the early jigsaw in place, we built plans to raise our initial seed capital, with a target of $10 million. This initial capital would allow us to hire staff, pay some accruing bills and start the build of the business, particularly the technology. We kicked the process off in early 2016 and worked hard over many months up to June 2016, calling on potential investors in Australia. We visited several private equity and venture capital funds, specialist investment funds and family offices.

We also spoke with three of the regional banks – Bendigo and Adelaide Bank, Bank of Queensland and Suncorp – and many others, as we felt then that these banks had arguably failed to make any meaningful progress in building SME franchises, and we thought they might be interested in investing in us. While we were able to get access at CEO level, the discussions were generally underwhelming and failed to gain much traction. We also spoke to Macquarie Bank, but again, several generally good meetings did not result in a productive outcome from our perspective.

In hindsight this was the best outcome for Judo, but at the time we were desperately looking for capital to keep the show on the road and build some momentum. We also believed that having a bank as a cornerstone shareholder would assist greatly in capital raising and getting to market sooner. Arguably it would have done, but it would have also brought a whole range of bureaucratic and legacy thinking, which may have stifled innovation and Judo's growth.

Will we survive?

Throughout the early stages, while the belief and passion continued to burn brightly, the hard reality was that the prospect of failure could not be dismissed. Few start-ups, if any, avoid facing those dreaded stages when it feels like everything is falling apart and the dream is turning into a nightmare. A range of emotions marched through our minds, not least of which was concern for the people that we had convinced to join the business – and then, of course, the financial loss that we and others would face. There were several times in our journey when it felt like the walls were closing in and we could feel the confidence of the team starting to fade, with some worry and anxiety starting to dominate discussions.

The first time we stared into that possibility of failure was when we struggled to raise seed capital. We faced it again when an investor pulled out of our major capital raise days before the Christmas break in 2017 – we discuss this horror moment later in this chapter.

How you lead through these dark moments is vital, even though the personal stress inevitably impacts sleep and mood. As we talk about in Chapter 7 on consciously building the culture of the company, you must be honest with everyone, but also positive. You have to remind everyone that we always expected dark moments, and that there is always more than one way to 'skin a cat'. You must also remind yourself and others that the euphoria of success is always hard-earned, and is sweeter because of the way in which difficult, business-threatening challenges are navigated. If it was easy, it wouldn't be worth doing; as Earl Campbell famously said, 'If it weren't for the dark days, we wouldn't know what it is to walk in the light'. You must keep visualising success. The old saying that 'leadership can be a lonely place' never felt truer than at the many times when the prospect of failure was looming.

Big breakthrough

Our first breakthrough came in July 2016, over dinner with Geoff Lord at Saké Restaurant & Bar at Southbank in Melbourne. We had known Geoff from our days at ANZ Bank and knew of his reputation as a serial entrepreneur. He was also a friend and had an uncanny eye for spotting business opportunities that few others see. Geoff clearly saw what we were seeking to build and how it could be successful. He tabled a proposal that was defining in Judo's success: he would arrange for a small group of his business associates to invest $5 million – if the Judo management team invested at least $1 million of new money over what had already been invested.

So started our capital raising. Geoff got his business associates together at his office just off St Kilda Road, and they listened diligently to our presentation. We knew the deal was close when one potential investor declared, 'Well, these fellows seem to know what they are talking about. I am in!' With management, Geoff and his associates, alongside several investors introduced by VentureCrowd in Sydney and Cambooya (Vincent Fairfax Family Office), became the founding investors in Judo. Without them it is highly likely Judo would never have got off the ground. In many ways, the difference between the investors that Geoff had assembled and the majority of those we had met and were to meet was that they were entrepreneurs – pioneering entrepreneurs. Experienced entrepreneurs can spot a good opportunity in a way that others cannot.

With the early capital in place, we started to hire critical staff and pay modest salaries to those in the business who had been working for nothing. We were also able to make a commitment to office space on a month-to-month arrangement in a Regus office set-up at Level 32, 367 Collins Street, Melbourne; we got a good rate because the ground floor and entrance to the building were about to undergo major reconstruction, so coming to work was going to involve walking through a building site.

Getting office space was an important practical and symbolic step up from the way we had operated for almost a year. Our modus operandi had been to meet at Strozzi on Collins Street and nurse a couple of coffees for a few hours, then make our way to The Langham hotel at Southbank and do the same. We would occasionally gatecrash Chris's apartment at Eureka Tower, and then Prima Pearl when he moved there. In Sydney, we would start at The Westin (now The Fullerton Hotel) on Martin Place and then find other locations to keep working without being asked to leave. Our good friend Steve Tucker, who ran the MLC business when it was part of NAB, offered us use of the Koda Capital offices at Circular Quay on the weekends. There we could assemble everyone and have detailed planning sessions, where we spent as much time on what Judo would *not* look and feel like – the bureaucratic 'mini-me' we describe in Chapter 9 – as on what it would. Team members in Melbourne flew up to Sydney at their own expense, as we had done when we visited Melbourne or, for that matter, anywhere, including our numerous trips to Beijing, Hong Kong, Singapore, Abu Dhabi, London and New York (which we go into later in the chapter).

Moving into a small office space at 367 Collins Street was a huge relief after a year of dodging the suspicious looks of staff across several coffee and hotel establishments in Melbourne and Sydney. Symbolically, of course, it helped make things feel real, and having everyone cramped in a small office space also engendered a sense of camaraderie. As numbers grew, we eventually moved to another modest office space at Southbank at an annual rental cost of $350,000.

As we grew, we closely managed our property costs so that in 2022, when we were in Sydney, Melbourne, Adelaide, Brisbane, Canberra, Newcastle, Geelong, Hobart and Perth, our aggregate costs were under $1.9 million. In contrast, when the failed neobank Xinja went out of business, its single property cost in Sydney alone was reportedly $1.7 million per annum.

With the seed capital in place, the pressure was on to get the larger sums of capital that the business needed. At least now we could point to some substance in terms of the people on the payroll and serious technology discussions that were now underway. Given that we were building the bank from a blank piece of paper, we needed people working on designing the IT, operations, risk management and all the other critical business frameworks, and doing so in a way that would satisfy the rigours of a banking licence application. (At that time, there was no documented road map for applying for a banking licence in Australia – it was one of the few things you couldn't google.) We could also pay some of the bills that had been contingent on the capital, so that we could ensure the ongoing goodwill of the professional advisors who had backed us at the outset.

However, raising serious amounts of capital for a bank start-up in Australia is no easy undertaking. By December 2016, we needed to raise additional seed capital to maintain momentum in building the business and to fund us through much of 2017, in anticipation of a major capital raise later that year. Through various networks, including Greg Ruddock at Ironbridge and family offices such as Cambooya (who have gone on to be one of our strongest and most supportive investors), we were able to raise a further $14 million, which included $6 million from the management team and qualifying employees. We were delighted that our people were willing to invest in the business. Of the $20 million we had raised at that stage, $7 million had come from the Judo team (not to mention the early funding, which was exclusively from the Judo team). That was real commitment, as many people had to remortgage their homes to make the investment. We never underestimated the significance of this – given the uncertainty that is associated with a start-up, adding financial leverage to the household balance sheet during an uncertain time was a bold move by some of our people and their families.

Major capital raisings, and building networks

The investor journey has been replete with learnings, which we attempt to consolidate in this chapter. Physically, it took us around the world six times and has been a journey that has continued to evolve, from the opening of our doors as a non-bank in April 2018, to the granting of our unrestricted banking licence in April 2019, through five capital-raising rounds, to our IPO on the Australian Securities Exchange in November 2021, and on from there.

Having completed the two phases of seed capital raising, we then turned our attention to planning our first large-scale capital raising. In early 2017, we made yet another trip to Beijing, Shanghai, Hong Kong, Singapore, Abu Dhabi and London. In London, we sought advice from John McFarlane, for whom we had both worked at ANZ and who was then Chairman at Barclays Bank. We met John over dinner at one of our favourite restaurants, Wiltons, on Jermyn Street. John's advice was resolute: 'You are either a scale player or a specialist player. If you are stuck in the middle, it's the worst of all worlds'. We also sought counsel from Mervyn Davies (Baron Davies of Abersoch), former Standard Chartered Bank Chairman and Trade Minister in Prime Minister Gordon Brown's government, and David Stileman at Corsair Capital on networks they had which might be interested in investing in Judo.

On every trip to London, one priority meeting was with Jonny Allison, a Managing Director at Macquarie Capital. Jonny had a first-class understanding of the challenger and neobank market in the UK and was a constant source of insight and advice. Disappointingly, while we had several conversations across different divisions of Macquarie in Australia, we were ultimately not able to leverage Jonny's engagement with his colleagues in Sydney into the broader and deeper domestic relationship we were looking for; but we are forever grateful for the quality of engagement with Jonny, who is a role-model banker.

The many meetings we crammed into a day saw us constantly travelling between the City of London, Mayfair and Canary Wharf. One memorable meeting we continue to reflect on was with Anthony Thomson. Anthony had been a co-founder of two UK challenger banks: Metro Bank and Atom Bank. He subsequently came to Australia and set up the neobank :86 400, with Robert Bell as the CEO. (:86 400 was acquired by NAB in 2021.) Anthony is a true entrepreneur, a 'PhD' in the science and craft of start-ups and a hugely impressive individual who, just like Joe Giannamore, does not pull his punches. His insights, advice and opinions are raw and unvarnished, but always constructive. After listening to our business thesis, he said that it sounded compelling, but in substance, all that we were describing was a 'faster horse!', or what Peter Thiel would describe as a 1 to n strategy. In other words, we were going to be faster and nimbler than the incumbents, but in his eyes that was not going to be enough: other, faster horses could soon emerge, and one or two of the Australian major banks might even learn to run faster (as unlikely as it might seem).

Anthony had a great point, and it caused us to reflect on the narrative and further critique and sharpen our emphasis on those points of competitive differentiation. We had been purposely downplaying our technology, particularly our philosophy of 'technology as a service' and our plans to develop machine-learning and AI capabilities as a basis for creating operational leverage and clear market differentiation. In part, our hesitation in promoting technology as a core business characteristic was due to a fear of being labelled or grouped as a 'fintech', which we thought would not do justice to the nature of the relationship-focused business we were building (and also because we envisioned the development of our technology as a multi-year journey). Anthony has been a great friend to Judo, agreeing on more than one occasion to come and address the Judo team, offering his insights and perspective on the journey that we were on. :86 400 and Judo were two very different business models serving two different segments of the market.

After meetings with Jerry del Missier (Copper Street Capital), Yanni Pipilis (SoftBank), former Westpac CEO Dr David Morgan AO (Chairman Europe and Asia Pacific at J.C. Flowers & Co.), Rishi Khosla (CEO at OakNorth Bank), former Midland Bank CEO Gene Lockhart, Caroline Woodworth (General Atlantic), Lindsey McMurray (Managing Partner, Pollen Street Capital) and many, many others, we then met with a range of smaller London-based banks, before circling back to Shawbrook and a meeting with their then-CEO Steve Pateman in their offices at Bishopsgate. We wanted to test whether any of the challenger banks would be interested in taking a cornerstone shareholding in Judo, a move which would further add to our credibility and ease the path to other sources of capital. Steve was interested. He understood the uncanny parallels between the UK and Australian banking markets, and he understood the investment thesis given his deep banking experience. He also had a soft spot for Australia, something we went on to find with several future investors – and not to be underestimated!

Over the course of the next four months, as discussions progressed in earnest, we put most of our eggs in the Shawbrook basket, because we saw it as a perfect fit. We had discussed them taking a 20 per cent stake and how we would work together to ensure that this was a strategic rather than simply financial relationship. With Shawbrook as a cornerstone investor, this would materially de-risk Judo in the eyes of investors and, ultimately, our soon-to-become regulator. Unfortunately, the deal collapsed due to the Shawbrook board's preference that the company focus on the UK market and not be distracted by opportunities over the other side of the world. The Shawbrook board had changed during our discussions, with two large private equity firms – Pollen Street Capital and BC Partners – having taken the company private again (having listed in 2015). This was a huge blow but a good lesson well learnt in not placing all your investment hopes in one major party. We had essentially lost an expensive four months in our capital raising journey: our fault, and emphatically not a criticism of Shawbrook, who conducted themselves professionally throughout and remain good friends.

By late 2017, our first major capital raise of $120 million was taking shape, but this had taken much longer than we had hoped and planned. Consequently, we were running out of seed capital and had to act. We decided to ask the senior team to forgo their salaries until the capital raising was complete. This step would ensure that we could continue to pay the rest of the staff. We were very mindful of the need to pay the rest of the team a working salary so they could live and pay for their commitments. We also set aside contingency funding from our own dwindling resources if it was needed to pay bills.

Having been hugely underwhelmed by the response of the Australian institutional market and finding a far more sophisticated and experienced reception from the offshore markets, we found ourselves spending an increasing portion of our time offshore. We returned to Abu Dhabi, Beijing, Shanghai, Hong Kong, Singapore, London and New York. We found London to be more fertile ground than New York in getting investor interest, even though in New York we met with many high-profile investors, such as Jeff Greenberg at Aquiline Capital Partners, George Soros's senior team and Kristofer Kraus from PIMCO. We would be disingenuous if we said that, at that point, we did not have fleeting concerns about pulling off the capital raise after the news from Shawbrook. We had met close to 100 potential investors, many of them several times, and had nothing to show for our efforts. However, the positive reframing of this is that, without necessarily realising it at the time, huge value had been created by that investment in establishing a network.

We were learning a lot. There was not one meeting that was a waste of time. We learnt how the market looks at start-ups of the kind we were canvassing (we come back to this later), how the international market thinks about Australia and, specifically, the questions and concerns investors had about our thesis. This was an invaluable feedback loop, and each evening, after a gruelling day, we would replay what we had heard and discuss what we had learnt. We then incorporated those areas of focus and learnings into detailed call notes, which we would circulate to our team and the board, and which were hugely useful when preparing for subsequent meetings with that investor. The old saying that feedback is a gift is so very true. Never waste that gift. That does not mean you have to agree with the feedback, but you must understand it and reflect on it.

Sitting out there in the market trying to raise capital for an extended period without success does create its own perception problems. There is a real risk that, just like the house that has been unsold for a long period in a bull market, people start to ask questions: 'What is wrong? Why isn't it selling?' The market starts to assume that there is an issue with the investment thesis that smart money has identified. The other question foreign investors naturally asked was, 'Why aren't Australian funds backing this?'

The value of strong advisors

One of the things that became evident to us as we planned our capital raising was that, while we had a reasonable network of investors, the potential investor universe for Judo was both far larger and more diverse by geography, fund type, investment mandate and investment size than we had initially appreciated. What also became equally clear was that identifying and accessing these investors was, in most cases, best done with the support and imprimatur of a capable advisor, but equally that no advisor was even close to being across the full list of potential investors.

Our initial use of advisors was during our seed capital raising, when we worked in well with a few smaller placement agents, including VentureCrowd in Sydney and Jonathan Scales of Jonnola Investments. They were in the majority tapping into high-net-worth individuals, as well as family offices, several of which went on to become material investors in subsequent rounds.

One of the things you realise clearly with the benefit of hindsight is the role luck plays in the path you end up travelling, though we subscribe to the Samuel Goldwyn saying 'The harder I work, the luckier I get'. In 2017, having completed our seed capital raising while preparing for our first full equity raising round, we had what turned out to be a particularly fortuitous meeting at an A-League soccer match in Sydney (Sydney FC were playing Western Sydney Wanderers FC). We ran into Seumas Dawes, the Chairman and Executive Director of Pepper Money, who we knew. We chatted briefly that evening, and during a subsequent follow-up he recommended we meet with Paul Buckley, who was a senior banker at Credit Suisse and then subsequently at Dresdner Bank, had gone on to found and run First Avenue Capital Partners in London.

We were planning yet another trip to London, so this was perfect timing. The meeting with Paul and the First Avenue team of Jonathan Davie and Nick Chronias at their offices just off Oxford Street in central London, and subsequently with Martin Donnelly back in Australia, was a game changer for us. They very quickly saw the opportunity and – after several weeks of detailed due diligence, including on us as individuals – agreed to act as an arranger. The First Avenue network is extensive, and they brought huge credibility to our proposition, gaining us access to investors that we would otherwise never have seen.

As our first major capital raising was entering its final phases, it was agreed that we would close it in two stages: stage one by 31 December 2017 for $60 million – six investors – and stage two by 31 March 2018. We were in good shape. Then, on 23 December 2017, one of those 'dark days' that Joe Giannamore warned us of dawned: one of the investors, a Melbourne-based Chinese investor who had committed $15 million, pulled out without any warning or explanation. This put the whole $120 million at risk, as other investors were likely to be spooked by such a sudden and unexplained withdrawal. We met with the representatives of the Chinese investor on Boxing Day to listen to concerns that, despite months of reassurance, were only now being tabled. There were no substantive issues, simply a change of mind (or a commitment that was never intended to be fulfilled – a textbook case of settlement risk).

We were furious. The team representing the investor were people that we had not met before, and to describe them as underwhelming would be generous. The sobering reality was that we had until 31 December – yes, probably the worst week of the year for this – to find another $15 million or the whole deal could be at risk. Thankfully, our colleague Mandy Jiang suggested we go back to Mr Li, who we had met in the initial stages of our fundraising. We had only six days, but they were the longest six days ever. Ultimately, after numerous meetings – including now infamous lunches, such as the one on 9 January 2018, when we saw a side of the otherwise health-conscious Chris Bayliss that hitherto had been kept a secret – we were able to give Mr Li the confidence he needed to step in and invest $15 million, and he agreed to do so through Zhong Yi Investment Pty Ltd. Perhaps it wasn't a miracle but, in a business sense, it was as close as it gets. It would have been so easy to collapse from exhaustion and frustration given the situation we were in, and given the terrible time of year from a business perspective, but with Mandy, Tim and Mal we worked nonstop to make sure that the first $60 million was agreed in principle by 31 December 2017, and it was!

However, the first phase of $60 million, which we called 'R1A', was not finalised until a meeting on 25 January 2018 (Australian businesses essentially close down for the first three weeks of January) at which Mr Li was introduced to other investors, including David Fite and Greg Ruddock from Ironbridge, and the teams from Abu Dhabi Capital Group (ADCG), Cambooya, Inception Asset Management and the Tang Family Office. It was to our great relief that that meeting went well, and so R1A was closed. R1B, which represented a further $60 million, was closed in April 2018 when OPTrust, Ironbridge Fund II, Credit Suisse Asset Management (based in New York, now SPF Investment Management), Myer Family Investments and Tikehau Capital became investors.

We should call out the important role played by David Fite, who is both an investor in and was then a Director of Judo (he resigned as a director at the time of the IPO in November 2021). David took a lead role in calming the nerves of the remaining investors in R1A and in smoothing the way for Mr Li to join the investment round. He did a fantastic job and, as a director of Judo Bank in its important formative years, he matched his reputation as a high-calibre individual with a first-class brain. He always asked the right questions, and he moved naturally between the dancefloor and the balcony with aplomb.

The journey to unicorn

Becoming a unicorn (a new business with an equity valuation of $1 billion) was a fantastic milestone. Our journey to that milestone began with our first major capital raise in late 2017 and early 2018, when we raised that first $120 million at a valuation of $120 million, with shares issued at $1. As the business developed and a banking licence was achieved in 2019, we raised a whopping $400 million at $1.40 per share, valuing the company at $650 million. Our third major capital raise of $228 million was undertaken in May 2020, right at the beginning of the COVID-19 crisis, with huge market uncertainty. We were delighted to get that issue away at $1.45 per share – no mean feat given bank stocks listed during COVID-19 had dropped by up to 30 per cent. This third capital raise took the valuation of the company to the magic $1 billion mark.

Subsequent capital raises were completed in December 2020 ($284 million at $1.75 per share, giving a $1.6 billion valuation) and in May 2021 ($124 million at $1.90 per share, giving a $1.9 billion valuation). That was our last equity raise as a private company. The next equity raise would be in November 2021, when we raised $350 million of 'new money' as part of our IPO at a price of $2.10, valuing the company at $2.3 billion. We discuss the IPO decision in Chapter 10, but the one thing we were very proud of regarding the listing valuation was that our initial seed and early-stage investors had more than tripled their money. Taking other people's money, for us, is one of the biggest responsibilities you can take on in business, and returning that money to them with adequate reward is something we took very seriously. We were also proud that we never had to undertake a 'down round' (issuing equity at a lower price than earlier raisings).

Major development

While we placed a significant emphasis on capital raising, we were heartened in May 2018 when the Australian government announced a commitment to open the banking system to new entrants in the form of a restricted banking licence regime. This was very similar to the framework in existence in the UK. Essentially, what it meant was that those applications meeting the standards prescribed by APRA could apply for a restricted licence, which would then be valid for two years. During that time, there was very limited scope for newly licensed banks to be active in the deposit market and to develop their business model. At the end of two years, either the entity had applied for and received a full banking licence or the business was wound down. In our discussions with APRA, the advice was that we should bypass the restricted licence regime and apply for an unrestricted or full banking licence, given the detailed business case work we had built, the experience of the management team and the financial resources that we had in place. During one memorable meeting with the APRA team, they said to us that they felt we were well advanced in being ready for the unrestricted application and the restricted system was not really designed for business cases such as ours.

Obtaining a banking licence, which was to become critical to our second major capital raise, is not an undertaking for the faint of heart. It is a hugely detailed and rigorous process spanning an extended period, and it is costly. We estimate that, ignoring the time involved (which was material), the direct and indirect costs of getting the application into its final form were in the order of between $5 million and $7 million. There is no criticism intended here, because obtaining a banking licence is a privilege and the requirements set by APRA are appropriate: they are detailed, rigorous and of a high standard, as they should be. The fact that three of the four banks that were issued a full licence in 2019 were no longer in business by early 2022 is not a reflection of the approach taken by APRA, who ensured that no depositor money was lost and had anticipated that some new entrants may not succeed. The failure of these new entrants can be understood by the absence of one or more of the 'three must-haves' discussed in Chapter 3.

Investing heavily in consistency

A great learning for us over time has been the incredible importance of consistency of engagement, of message and of progress. It is something we have invested heavily in, and we cannot overstate the importance of this.

About halfway through a meeting in 2019 with a potential investor who we had seen several times in London since 2016, he held his hand up, pulled out another of his notebooks, flicked back through it and, looking up at us, said, 'You guys are saying exactly the same thing as you did two-and-a-half years ago!' We looked at each other as if that should be a surprise, and he added, 'You'd be surprised just how rare that is'.

This feedback highlights one of the strongest learnings of our capital raising journey, that of the credibility gained by delivering a clear and consistent message over time. The ability to sit across the table two or three times a year over several years and say 'This is what we said we would do, and this is what we have done' progressively builds a familiarity with the business, a sense of confidence in the consistency of focus and a track record of self-imposed waypoints measuring our successes and shortcomings. This, in turn, builds a solid base of confidence over time in our capacity to execute.

Every investor is unique – be prepared

From our first meetings onward, we always prepared carefully – reviewing call notes from any previous meetings, seeking to anticipate the key areas investors would press into and the questions they would ask, and ensuring to the greatest extent possible we had clear and succinct answers. We also had a policy of no BS: if we did not know the answer, then we would say so and come back with the answer.

Experienced investors, by virtue of the number of pitches they see, have highly tuned 'BS meters', and occasionally saying you don't know something adds credibility rather than detracting from it. So, our strong advice is to be absolutely straight in answering all questions.

Importantly, this regular, open and transparent approach to dealing with investors is now hardwired into Judo. Many of our investors have remarked on how fundamentally different their ongoing engagement with Judo is compared with other investee companies in their portfolio: more frequent, with a real depth of conversation and a consistent responsiveness to questions or requirements.

The value of creating such a solid base of goodwill is not to be underestimated. The inevitable problems get raised earlier and solved more easily. Also, 90 per cent of our larger investors (up until the IPO) invested in Judo over multiple rounds, and a material number of investors were referred to us by existing investors.

Of course, every one of the close to 100 investors we spent time with is unique. They have differing areas of industry expertise, differing mandates, differing geographic market focuses, and different backgrounds and experiences. What we have found over time, though, is that, when you combine that multitude of different investor types and attitudes with regular engagement and progressively deepening familiarity and knowledge, what occurs is a natural 'self-selection' or 'self-sorting' of investors. Some emerge as having the risk appetite to join in the early rounds, while others require additional 'proof points' along the journey before they join (with the understanding that, as the risks come down, so do the returns – but that's OK because it fits their specific risk appetite): 'Come back to me when you've got your banking licence'; 'Come back to me when you've lent your first dollar/taken your first deposit/turned your first monthly profit'; and so on.

By way of example, at one end of the spectrum we had a substantial and highly sophisticated investor who contacted us a fortnight before the closing of our first major capital raising to say they'd like to look at participating. Given the due diligence being done by other investors in the round, many of whom had been working on the raise for six months, we explained that the close on 21 April 2018 was a hard close and that we could not extend. 'No problem,' they said. To our amazement, and their credit, they completed their due diligence inside two weeks and became a key investor in that and in many of our subsequent capital raisings. We also had one substantial investor who said that they were investing because of the management team ('the jockey') and did not need to conduct further due diligence!

At the other end of the spectrum, two of our UK-based investors – who we began talking to in 2016 and visited upwards of ten times, who got to know us inside out and observed our delivery against our own self-imposed 'waypoints' – became first-time and significant investors in our fourth major capital raising four years later.

Shoe leather, critical qualities and sage advice

Put simply, in seeking investors we found there is just no substitute for 'wearing out shoe leather', or, to borrow from a parallel idea from the book *Blown to Bits* by Philip Evans and Thomas Wurster, it's about 'richness and reach'. 'Richness' in this case is the combination of the depth and quality of the engagement you can achieve, and the personal relationship, rapport and credibility you are able to build over time when you are physically sitting across the table. 'Reach' is all about the number of qualified investors you see and the consistency with which you see them.

In the period from 2015 to 2019, that's exactly what we did. We made numerous international trips, and invested heavily in building relationships and rapport with investors and progressively developing their familiarity with the Judo proposition.

One of our more significant frustrations in having to make these trips during our first several rounds of capital raising was facing the questions, 'Where are the Australian investors? What do they know that we don't?' It is an unfortunate irony that, while the Australian financial system is one of the deepest in the world, when it came to raising capital for a new Australian bank serving Australian SMEs, most of our capital in our first several rounds came from international investors.

On richness

Perhaps in the post-COVID-19 world, a greater proportion of capital will be raised through remote and virtual connection – that's how our IPO process was conducted, as described in Chapter 10. For us, though, we have always felt that, in the vast majority of circumstances, the richness of conversation that comes with face-to-face meetings creates the strongest and most durable foundation with investors.

As a cornerstone, it allowed us to frame the conversations around the strength of our sense of purpose and belief, something that is established far more through tone, body language and personal chemistry than it is through words. It also allowed us to establish 'across the table' that, for example, risk management was a central plank in every dimension of how we were building Judo and that we were across it.

We also knew that each conversation has two distinct and roughly equal elements:

1. **The commercial opportunity:** The nature of the proposition and the risk–return trade-off over time.
2. **An assessment of us as individuals:** It does not take mind-reading powers to know that every potential investor was thinking, 'OK, I get the business opportunity, I buy the proposition, but can these guys and their team pull it off? Can they execute?'

This reinforces the point made in Chapter 1 that the calibre of management is so important in the way that investors assess opportunities. As Thomas Eisenmann observed, management's industry expertise considerably reduces start-up risk. That expertise needs to be deep, not superficial. Far too many people pass themselves off as experienced in an area when, on close examination, their experience is narrow and shallow. The 'jockey' matters more than the 'horse'!

To that end, in our initial meetings with a prospective investor we always spent the opening minutes introducing ourselves, our backgrounds, the genesis of Judo, the background and calibre of the leadership team we had put together, and then, later in the meeting, the depth and experience of the board.

A key learning along the way was that, with a significant portion of investors, you must work to keep yourselves top of mind given the volume of propositions they typically review. So, from early on we decided not just to visit at points when we were raising capital but to maintain consistency of contact between raises, both face-to-face and with regular video-conference calls, to update them around key achievements: for example, obtaining our banking licence, our first wholesale funding facility or our first $1 billion of lending.

Supplementing that consistent engagement, from our first capital raise onward we have always had behind us a comprehensive, up-to-date and well-organised virtual data room. This allowed those investors whose interest we had captured and their analyst teams to immediately go in and start looking at the detail behind the discussion.

Perhaps as clear a proof point as any of the value of the strong and durable foundation these many face-to-face and follow-up meetings between 2015 and 2020 created was the fact that, during the COVID-19-driven disruption to markets in 2020 and 2021, when there was no travel and no face-to-face meetings, we raised more than $500 million in capital at progressively higher prices.

On reach

We simply did the miles. The typical trip for us involved flying out of Sydney on a Sunday and doing a mix of Beijing, Shanghai, Hong Kong and Singapore on the Monday, Tuesday and Wednesday; then on to Abu Dhabi at the back end of the week; on to London, getting in Saturday night for a quick pint or two at The King William IV or The Flask and staying until Wednesday; New York Thursday and Friday; then back to Australia over the weekend. To say this schedule was gruelling is an understatement, but it is part of the price you must pay when living in Australia – the tyranny of distance.

Travel is a bit like what John Wanamaker (the founder of Macy's in the USA) said about advertising in the late 1800s: 'Half the money I spend on advertising is wasted; the trouble is I don't know which half'.

And so, with investor meetings, quite simply it is about the grind: you travel the miles, and you take the meetings. Unlike with Macy's advertising, it is true with investors that you do find out in the end who turns up, but a common theme is that there are always surprises. We worked out quickly that approximately 50 per cent of those we saw never really intended to invest, but took the meeting because they were interested in hearing what the sector was doing and how new entrants were approaching it as background or benchmark-setting for existing investments in their portfolio. Equally, there were numerous meetings we left thinking there was a low probability of any follow-on, only to have the investor come back and begin to do serious work on the company. There were also those whose commitment we felt sure of who pulled out at a minute to midnight (literally).

You can pick some, but there are also many you can't. Also, as highlighted earlier, they may be a no today but a yes in a future round, or you may find they say at the end, 'This isn't for me, but I want to introduce you to…'

On clarity

With clarity, it's about continuously working on it.

One of the great benefits of speaking with investors as a team was the ability to critique each other's delivery. It was also an opportunity to sit back at some point in the meeting and observe the body language of those across the table – was the message being heard and understood? Were we getting the cut-through? As Peter Drucker famously said, 'The most important thing in communication is to hear what isn't being said'.

Between meetings we would regularly download and do a self-critique over a coffee or sandwich to assess the meeting: our delivery, the clarity of our message, our responses to questions, whether we prejudged what we thought they were asking, what the emergent themes were at a macro level and how they tied in with issues other investors were raising.

A great learning here for us, and indeed anyone that embarks on this pitching process, was to embed the meeting review as a discipline, and from that, actively evolve your approach – not your message, your approach – and your effectiveness in delivering it.

Our experience was also that you are better off *not* talking to a PowerPoint deck. To some this may not appeal, as it is for many presenters the default setting, and in many ways it's the easiest (read: laziest). Our experience over hundreds of meetings was that a well-planned, crisp and interactive conversation had by far the greatest impact. For clarity, this does not mean that you shouldn't have a deck; however, do take the time to make the deck short but comprehensive, conveying important concepts while at the same time being easy and intuitive to read. Our advice is to keep the deck to under ten slides and anchor the discussion on one or two slides, which you might reference in the discussion to help bring key points to life.

Take the time. For us, many of the presentations began as 30 pages and ended up as six or seven. We also got into the habit of handing out the deck well through the meeting and only as needed, and in many cases we only handed it out as we were leaving.

Again, don't talk to it; if you need to refer to the deck to illustrate a point, so be it, but the words 'page turn' should never be uttered. You should know your stuff, almost like getting ready to sit an exam, and not need to turn to textbooks or notes except to reinforce or illustrate a key point.

On flexibility and resilience

Another thing we learnt along the way was to be prepared to flex our delivery style and content based on the wide range of investors we met, and the responses (both verbal and nonverbal) we received.

Our experience of investors was that there were several continuums:

- from the most hardened and immovable sceptic, to the investor that nods after five minutes and says, 'I get it, yes I get it… exactly what the market is screaming out for'
- from investors who span multiple industries and need an explanation of key concepts, to the highly industry-literate
- from those that are straight into the micro, to those that leave the detail to be examined between meetings and remain focused on the strategic conversation
- from those who are focused on the price from meeting one, where it's all about 'getting something cheap', to those who prefer to get to know the company first, and only after deciding to proceed then focus on appropriate pricing and expected returns (lean to the latter every time)

- from investors who are consistently understated around any potential commitment, to those who say 'You don't need to see anyone else, we'll do the whole thing' within the first half an hour – a real case for us that set alarm bells ringing early in the conversation.

These are simply our own observations and are not intended to be comprehensive, nor is any editorial comment intended: investors are not right or wrong in their approach. The list simply underscores the diversity of perspectives we encountered, the need to remain flexible, and that the fact sticking to a rigid presentation format materially reduces the effectiveness of your engagement.

We are also great believers in these words of the ancient Greek philosopher Epictetus: 'We have two ears and one mouth so that we can listen twice as much as we speak.' You learn a lot when you listen, and not much when you are doing all the talking!

On Australia as an investment destination

While at the macro level Australia is globally recognised as a sophisticated market, we regularly faced a key challenge: the 'tyranny of distance', the practical difficulty and time required to come to Australia, walk the offices, meet the staff and see the operations. Secondly as one New York–based fund manager pointed out, 'Australia represents less than 2 per cent of global GDP, so that's roughly how much time I spend thinking about it.' It was said tongue-in-cheek, but the message was a real one. For a material number of our investors, Judo has been their first investment in Australia, and part of their due diligence included building a foundational understanding of the market, investment landscape and economic outlook.

A counterpoint to these challenges, discovered along the way, was the significant value of individuals having an affiliation with

Australia or New Zealand. Those affiliations included having worked here for a period, having a family member or close friend living here, having personally completed a degree at an Australian or New Zealand university or having a family member currently completing one. In one case, the investor owned a property in Queenstown, New Zealand – we could almost see him thinking that another three hours to Queenstown after a 24-hour flight to Melbourne would be easy!

*

In summary, Judo's journey with investors in many ways parallels our proposition to the SME market. We have worked hard over many years to partner with a diverse set of investors, building progressive depth in those relationships through a consistent, open and constructive engagement from both sides of the table. We were always guided by the old saying, 'Tell me who your friends (investors) are, and I will tell you who you are!'

Success in capital raising and in building a business requires incredible stamina and belief that it can be done. It also requires limitless persistence (or resilience)! Former US President Calvin Coolidge summarised this perfectly when he said:

> 'Nothing in the world can take the place of persistence. Talent will not; nothing is more common than unsuccessful men with talent. Genius will not; unrewarded genius is almost a proverb. Education will not; the world is full of educated derelicts. Persistence and determination alone are omnipotent. The slogan "Press on!" has solved and always will solve the problems of the human race.'

7

Finding our balance

Building the team and culture

A deep-seated belief we held about the bank we wanted Judo to become was the principle that it would be our human and cultural capital, more than financial capital, that would define our success over time. We knew that an early test of the attractiveness of what we wanted to build was going to be our ability to convince the people we wanted to work with us to leave the security of their hard-earned status at larger organisations. We also knew that these are not just decisions made by an individual: they are very often family decisions (as they should be), which can involve dealing with much uncertainty on the part of the spouse, partner or family members not directly involved. Explaining that you are leaving your 10- or 20-year career at a major bank to join Judo Bank would, in many cases, have provoked the response, 'Judo who? And what about the financial security of our family?' The reality is that Australia and New Zealand are such shallow markets for good roles in banking (senior executive roles, full stop!) that people understandably hang on when they attain such a role, often counting down the years to when financial security – aided sometimes by a large and accruing termination cheque – provides escape and the liberty to do other, more gratifying things in what are often the early autumn years of life. It takes a particular confidence and risk appetite to move from the constant warm-bath comfort of the establishment to a start-up. It takes an entrepreneurial mindset for the founders and a founder-centric mindset for those who follow at a later stage as the business grows in scale.

Just as we had taken care in developing a purpose statement for the business, we also thought long and hard about the purpose statement for our people: what was our vision when it came to people and culture? (This, again, is often glossed over by entrepreneurs and viewed as 'big corporate' spin, which is understandable, because many big corporations have changed their purpose statements dozens of times.) We have a very strong view on this, particularly given that we were hiring in an industry that had lost the trust and passion of so many of its people. We developed the following employee purpose statement based on input from colleagues, including our then People & Culture Head Megan Collins, and Steve Mifsud, who headed our business in NSW and Canberra:

> To be the most trusted employer in Australian business banking, full of employees who are raving fans, working in the best job they've ever had!

Flowing from that purpose statement was a ten-point employee value proposition (EVP), built in very much the same way as the detailed customer value proposition. We have always believed that if you hire well, people do not need to be micromanaged, and most do not want that anyway. Good people want the freedom and trust to get on with their job and work collaboratively with colleagues. As Steve Jobs famously said, 'It doesn't make sense to hire smart people and tell them what to do; we hire smart people so they can tell us what to do.'

One of the benefits of having deep industry experience and being reasonably well-known in an industry is not only the knowledge of the essential skills needed to build and run a bank, but also a good understanding of the talent in the market. The reputation of the founder team can be critical here. All the original founders brought exceptional talent into the business. If the founders are well-known and have had demonstrable career success and good reputations, then their ability to attract talent is a lot better than someone new to the industry. Knowing the banking business and industry inside out gave us a very clear sense of not just the technical skills we would need but the cultural fit that we were looking for.

In essence, we were looking for what Carol Dweck, in her book *Mindset*, calls a 'growth mindset'. She describes people with a growth mindset as:

> '... constantly monitoring what's going on, but their internal monologue is not about judging themselves and others in this way. Certainly, they're sensitive to positive and negative information, but they're attuned to its implications for learning and constructive action.'

We also wanted our senior people to be self-starters and comfortable with ambiguity. It was important that the senior people joining us early understood that a start-up is, in essence, a huge experiment that may not work, so their personal qualities around thriving in uncertainty were going to be fundamental. Titles, job descriptions and functional boundaries were the last thing we wanted to think about in the early years, even though we knew we would have to eventually.

We wanted people who could care deeply about what we were building and the vision we had. The moment you feel the need to tightly manage someone and have lost confidence in their judgement, you have made a hiring mistake (or your management style needs to be assessed). This is not to say that weekly, fortnightly or monthly catchups are not important – they are – but some managers find it hard to give their people the room to get on with their job and use their initiative with confidence. We wanted a culture of freedom within defined values and strategic boundaries. We also believe in the adage that A-grade people attract other A-grade people, while 'B's' often attract 'C's' but never 'A's'.

We wanted people who were just as passionate as we were about the purpose and values we had defined Judo by. As Simon Sinek puts it in his book *Leaders Eat Last*, 'If you hire people just because they can do a job, they'll work for your money. But if you hire people who believe what you believe, they'll work for you with blood, sweat, and tears'. High-performing people and teams need a sense of meaningfulness, a sense of purpose. This is particularly true of people with the entrepreneurial 'gene'. There are some important differences between the type of people who thrive in a large bureaucracy and those that crave a more entrepreneurial setting. This is an important lens in hiring people and in shaping the culture that you want the organisation to be defined by.

We wanted people with an entrepreneurial 'gene', people who would find strong personal alignment between the company we wanted to build and the company that they wanted to be part of. Given the nature of bureaucracy within the banking industry – and, indeed, inside many large businesses – we believed that there was not a deep pool of such people. To our delight and relief, we were wrong! People want to belong to an organisation that aligns to their natural values, and where they can feel happy, challenged and good about themselves. As Steve Jobs said, 'Your work is going to fill a large part of your life, and the only way to be truly satisfied is to do what you believe is great work. And the only way to do great work is to love what you do'.

Joining an entrepreneurial firm in a staid industry is not for everyone. It is a roller-coaster ride, with high levels of ambiguity, job uncertainty in the early stages, long hours and real pressure to deliver with nowhere to hide. Then add to that the real prospect of failure.

People with an entrepreneurial 'gene' ride the roller-coaster and feel that the highs of building something new compensate for the stress and anxiety of the occasional lows. This is because they thrive in an environment where there is a strong alignment between themselves and the business purpose.

In a detailed, multi-country study of this phenomenon, researchers put this down to three psychological factors. The first factor is a sense of purposeful engagement in an environment free from the stifling bureaucracy that Hamel and Zanini describe in their book *Humanocracy*, where so much of what is done is subject to layers of policies and other rules. Such organisations have more 'blockers' than 'attackers', and most staff can't relate to the customers that the business is there to serve. The second factor is a sense that there is a greater use of their capabilities and interests, in contrast to an environment where the forces that block progress outweigh the forces for change and innovation, often by a ratio of three to one. In an engaging and aligned environment, they feel stretched, fulfilled and growing. The third factor is a feeling of themselves developing strength and resilience as they adapt and thrive in the roller-coaster ride, often looking back with pride and occasionally astonishment at how much they have achieved, despite the hurdles and despite the ambiguity.

In combination, these factors mean that people with the entrepreneurial 'gene' frequently associate their identity with their job. They perceive themselves as pursuing a destiny or a calling, rather than simply having a job as a 'hired hand'; and this leads to an enhanced state of physical and mental wellbeing, which is essential to the effectiveness of motivation, creativity and getting things done. This sense of meaningfulness is critical in any start-up, particularly as so many of the tasks that must be completed can be mundane in nature, and everyone must be a jack-of-all-trades. Where there is a sense of meaningfulness, such mundane tasks do not have that sense of drudgery.

Building an organisation and building a business are two different things

Conscious of Joe Giannamore's early counsel, we knew that just as important as recruiting A-graders was hiring people who could embrace agility and cope with the ambiguity of a start-up. This is not for everyone: not everyone is comfortable with uncertainty and risk, as Tara Swart et al describe in the excellent book *Neuroscience for Leadership*. Mental and emotional agility are crucial leadership competences.

Together with the capacity to deal with ambiguity is the absolute importance of having the conversations that need to be had, and doing so in a way that is constructive and not personal. We talk about this 'point easy' concept in more detail in Chapter 8, but it is summarised well by Susan Scott in her excellent book *Fierce Conversations*, in which she says, 'Remember that what gets talked about and how it gets talked about determines what will happen. Or won't happen. And that we succeed or fail, gradually then suddenly, one conversation at a time.' It's easy to say that you should have candid, constructive conversations, but in practice not everyone is comfortable having those conversations. There are also those who suffer 'amygdala hijacks', where their interpretation of events causes a fight-or-flight response, which is often counterproductive.

In addition to interviewing for the ability to deal with ambiguity, and to constructively advocate a view or position, we always used our values to screen people. Does your instinct say you can trust this person? Are they a team player? Are they someone who enjoys accountability? Are they someone who wants to be a high performer? How will they cope with ambiguity? Are they a 'We' person or an 'I' person? What we did not want was people who operate like Robinson Crusoe: poor communicators who hold things to themselves, people who are steeped in and highly adept at the craft of internal political behaviour, which is so often evident in large organisations. This is not to say that we wanted a tension-free team environment; there are always going to be tensions, and in fact you want that, because it lifts the quality of debate and decision-making if managed in a mature, ethical, authentic and transparent manner.

The evolving nature of critical skills

We knew that, as the business grew, the mix of skills and experience needed would continuously evolve. One key piece of early advice – but one that would never change – was the need for strong alignment with our purpose and values.

Accepting that some people who were essential to the building of the bank might not be the right people to help grow and manage the bank was not easy. This is a common problem with successful start-ups: sometimes the organisation's needs outgrow the capabilities of individuals, and it is often very difficult to say to colleagues who have been with you from the beginning as part of a founding team, and who you consider friends, that the time for them to move on has come. Difficult as these conversations are, they can also be critical to the business's success. The challenge we faced in having these discussions with our colleagues was in explaining, and having them understand, that the change had nothing to do with their performance, while acknowledging the understandable emotional reaction from the colleague, who would feel that there was a more sinister underlying reason when there was not.

Equally, some people do not enjoy the more disciplined management and governance processes that come with a growing business, or the nature of regulation, which can be the antithesis of entrepreneurialism. An example of this was highlighted when the founder of UK challenger bank Monzo, Tom Blomfield, announced his departure from the bank. As the bank was growing, Tom had become disillusioned and unhappy in his role as CEO. He said:

> 'I stopped enjoying my role probably about two years ago… as we grew from a scrappy startup that was iterating and building stuff people really love, into a really important U.K. bank. I'm not saying that one is better than the other, just that the things I enjoy in life is working with small groups of passionate people to start and grow stuff from scratch, and create something that customers love. And I think that's a really valuable skill but also taking on a bank that's three, four, five million customers and turning it into a 10 or 20 million customer bank and getting to profitability and IPOing it, I think those are huge, exciting challenges, just honestly not ones that I found that I was interested in or particularly good at.'

We were also very concerned that, if we were to adopt conventional management practices (those that we were schooled in), there was a real risk of suffocating the fledgling business with unproductive or 'bad' bureaucracy – exactly the kind of reason why our new and talented employees were leaving their existing employers. Consistent with the frustrations echoed by Tom Blomfield, Jim Collins wrote in his book *Good to Great* about the outcomes of emergent bureaucracy:

> '"This isn't fun anymore, I used to be able to just get things done. Now I must fill out these stupid forms and follow these stupid rules." The creative magic begins to wane, as some of the most innovative people leave… The exciting start up transforms into just another company.'

Perhaps the biggest insight from Blomfield and Collins is that there is a big difference between building an organisation and building a business. As start-up businesses grow, there comes a point when the priority must move to building an organisation that will allow the business to scale. There is no getting away from the reality that, as businesses grow, complexity sets in. Complexity, if not managed well, will allow bureaucracy to take root. Most entrepreneurs are great at launching a business, but few are great at building an organisation. Many founding entrepreneurs struggle to manage the transition to a larger, more complex business, and to manage the many risks that such a transition entails. There is an adage with start-ups that 'founders can't scale'. This view is largely based on the premise that, as a company grows, the founders lack the competencies to manage an organisation and a leader with a traditional management background is needed.

Sometimes it can be the ego of the founders that is the problem. They can't come to terms with the reality that the business's needs are now more important than their leadership style, and the strength and cohesion of the management is more important than any one individual. Few entrepreneurs can detach their ego from their business, and thus they continue to try and dominate when the business needs a strong, broad-based team at the top more than a dominating leader.

The reality is that many entrepreneur founders (as Tom Blomfield might be) don't enjoy the idea of building an organisation. They are captivated by the new product and its prospects, and ultimately about making it profitable. While people are always important, the founders can assume that people 'get it', and being part of building something is enough motivation to underpin buy-in. This can be a big mistake. As businesses grow, people management becomes the critical success factor. This is where most entrepreneurs come unstuck: they fail to build a people-centric organisation. As organisational design becomes more complex, there is a need to finetune, and sometimes revamp, the way the business operates internally and how that is linked to the external environment. The external environment often dictates much of internal reality. We come back to this important dynamic in Chapter 9.

The right mix

We would regularly talk about the mix of expertise that we had assembled and ask ourselves, 'Who can build the business with an entrepreneurial mindset, and are they also capable of building an organisation as we look to scale?' Given that all the founding leadership team came from the banking industry, there was a lingering concern that the dominant DNA would be to avoid risk rather than sensibly embrace and manage it. We would regularly position our leadership on a risk appetite–risk aversion scale and ask ourselves, 'Do we have the right balance for the current needs of the business?'

We do not mean to suggest that any position on the risk scale is better than any other. The key is the balance in the team. Having too many key founders with a high-risk *appetite* could lead to problems, if not failure, but so could having the balance in the team weighted too heavily towards high-risk *aversion* (even though it is the dominant trait of bank executives, as it should be). As you move from building a business to building a scalable organisation, there is always a need revisit the mix, and this often means bringing in senior hires and having to inform founders that the needs of the organisation have changed. Banking, as a high-risk and heavily regulated industry, would require the balance to move towards high-risk aversion as the business scales.

We talked a lot about the importance of being comfortable with operational risk as we built the business, regularly using the metaphor of 'laying the tracks after the train had left the station' – something that would never be tolerated in more mature organisations, nor as the business moved into a more regulated environment. However, we had to accept and manage that risk if we were going to get the show on the road; the key was to make sure that the tracks were being laid faster than the speed of the travelling train. We had seen too many new banks (and, indeed, other companies) take forever to get to market, and sometimes fail as a result, because they ran out of money. So, another piece of advice is to accept some operational risk in getting to market, but be clear on that risk and how it is to be managed, and have contingency plans in place. This goes back to our points made earlier about really critiquing the business model, and measuring twice and cutting once.

Organisational design

Another important feature of building an organisation is how it is designed. Again, some entrepreneurs may view this as 'big corporate' management thinking and unnecessary bureaucracy, yet it can play a crucial role in how the business is led, its preparedness for scale and how its culture evolves. What you do in early years can be defining. Here, a top-quality Human Resources (HR) or People and Culture (P&C) executive is a must. Most start-ups would baulk at the thought of hiring a top-class HR executive, but if the intention is to scale the business then such an appointment can make a big difference. Such a person will guide thinking on organisational design, hiring plans and remuneration structures. Probably most importantly, such a person will provide advice on how to build, strengthen and preserve the culture within the organisation. A top-class HR executive becomes a critical and essential advisor to the founders and the CEO of the business. It is an essential role, and we were delighted to have identified an outstanding individual in Megan Collins to take on such a critical strategic position within the leadership team.

We made a conscious decision from the outset that Judo would not be a division-based or geography-based organisation. While we had different geographic locations, we would run only one profit and loss (P&L), and we emphasised the 'one Judo team'. We wanted colleagues in different locations to think of themselves as on different floors in the same building and work collaboratively across each team;

this is an example of the kind of practical, real-world embedding of the culture and EVP in the day-to-day working of the business that we discussed in previous chapters. This is, however, easier said than done, as all our bankers had come from large institutions where divisional and business unit P&Ls – and, sometimes, internal rivalry – were the norm. The importance of internal networking (and not in the sense of sucking up to senior people) is central to teamwork and productivity. It is vital to building the social fabric of an organisation, particularly in a start-up. The most important networks are those formed by employees across multiple functions that are creating things for the business or solving problems that require a truly enterprising lens. (This is not about open-plan offices, which are much overhyped in terms of what they bring to a business's productivity, let alone creativity.) This approach is at the centre of an agile business, with enterprise-wide teams assembled to tackle operational and strategic issues.

As discussed, while we built out the organisational design, we sought to continually evolve and improve that design over time. A topic of constant vigilance was the avoidance of allowing the seeds of 'bad' bureaucracy to take root. Instead, we very much subscribed to the philosophy of Hamel and Zanini in *Humanocracy*, which convincingly argues that it is possible to capture the benefits of bureaucracy – control, consistency and coordination – while avoiding the negative costs: inflexibility, mediocrity and disengagement. The key is to build a human-centric organisation. Our estimate is that 'bad' bureaucracy – which Hamel and Zanini describe as 'the top-down, rule-choked management structure that undergirds virtually every organisation on the planet' – covers 25 to 30 per cent of the operating costs within many large banks, a high level of unproductive costs not transparent in blunt CTI measures. As Hamel and Zanini summarise:

> 'Our organisations are failing us. They're sluggish, change-phobic, and emotionally arid. Human beings, by contrast,

are adaptable, creative, and full of passion. This gap between individuals and organizational capability is the unfortunate by-product of bureaucracy.'

Learning, unlearning and relearning

One of the central applications of that agile and adaptive thinking was the building of a challenger and founder-centric mindset within a senior team that had predominantly come from the major banks. Experience is essential in building a new bank, but in growing and differentiating the bank, there was a real risk of legacy thinking getting in the way. The more someone is trained and experienced in doing things, the more they become locked in a habit or behaviour pattern that is deeply stored in different parts of the brain, and the more they unconsciously plant the seeds of that behaviour in those around them. To change these beliefs, behaviours and habits is not easy. The concept of neuroplasticity is important in understanding adult learning, and how people can change the way they think about things and replace deeply held schemata on how things work. We think the following unattributed quote sums up the challenge: 'The illiterate of the 21st century won't be those who can't read and write, but those who can't learn, unlearn and relearn'.

For those committed to unlearning and relearning, understanding how neuroplasticity works is key. An important and relevant theory is Hebbian theory (or Hebb's rule), named after Canadian psychologist Donald Hebb, who argued that a learning depends on the plasticity of circuits in the brain caused by neurons making new synaptic transmissions with other neurons. By reinforcing these connections, new learning occurs as 'neurons that fire together, wire together'. These neuroscientific insights are thematically consistent with Malcolm Gladwell's *Outliers*, wherein Gladwell argues that mastery of a skill is in large part a function of the investment of 10,000 hours of learning. We are passionate about the importance of lifelong learning and have worked to weave that into the fabric of Judo, such as through having the leadership of the company all complete the MIT Sloan School of Management course on 'Neuroscience for Leadership', as well as our commitment to the professional values of the Chartered Banker Institute as administered by the Financial Services Institute of Australasia (FINSIA).

We are great believers in keeping abreast of high-quality and rigorously researched thinking in business practices, as occasionally you can come across an insight or perspective that influences the way you think about an important issue or opportunity. From the outset of Judo, we have been circulating articles, videos and online posts of all kinds; it has become an integral and enjoyable part of the organisation's continuous learning. Sometimes you can come across game-changing ideas and insights. This is so important in a fast-changing business, society and geopolitical environment. Our culture at Judo, and one of the components of that carefully crafted EVP, is the encouragement and funding of professional and personal development, whether that is through professional education or more general leadership education. One of our all-time favourite quotes on the importance of staying informed came from an advertisement for *The Economist* that read, '"I Have Never Read *The Economist*." – management trainee, aged 42'. The key point here is that the brain is both agile and resilient, and leadership must see how neuroplasticity can play a role in creating a highly effective leadership team and the agile and adaptive mindset required to flourish in Judo, regardless of age. Lifelong learning is just so important. There are two books in particular, which we reference regularly, that have influenced much about how we think about teamwork, having seen so many dysfunctional teams elsewhere. The first is *The Wisdom of Teams* by Jon R Katzenbach and Douglas K Smith, and the second is *Multipliers*, by Liz Wiseman.

Migrant mindset

As Judo grew, we asked everyone who joined to write a one-page 'Who Am I?' statement. This was their life story on a page, and its contents were up to them. When we went through the first 50 'Who Am I?' statements, we saw that most of our people had a rural upbringing, attended non-sandstone universities, had first-generation-immigrant parents, had achieved progress in life often due to the sacrifices of their parents, and were hungry to achieve in life. Naturally, there were exceptions to this, but there was a common theme that started to define the type of people we were attracting, who were thriving in the Judo environment and, therefore, were the type of people we wanted to attract.

As we looked at these emerging themes, the phrase 'migrant mindset' captured the essence of what we were seeing and what appealed to us. Modern Australia, New Zealand, the USA and Canada are great countries that were built through the ingenuity of migrants. We found our connection with Joseph Assaf – who we knew well through his leadership of the Ethnic Business Awards (EBA) – continually coming up in conversation. The EBA is an annual event that recognises the best Australian SMEs founded by immigrants to the country, and we found that there was a large commonality in those that were thriving within Judo with so many of the characteristics we saw in those migrant entrepreneurs. So, we started to define a typical Judo employee as having a 'migrant mindset' with eight common characteristics:

1. Resilient
2. Hungry
3. Inquisitive
4. Energetic
5. Decisive
6. Courageous
7. Passionate
8. Adaptive.

These characteristics became part of the screening process we used in hiring: we would look for strong evidence of at least six of the eight in prospective employees.

Now, this is not to say that we have not hired those from the sandstone universities – we have a fair number of Melbourne Business School MBAs in our ranks – or from more establishment backgrounds, but it does send a message about the general characteristics we are looking for in someone joining the 'Judo Family': we want challengers! We want people with real hunger, burning ambition and a migrant mindset – people who know that success only comes as a function of their hard work, not from the silver spoon and smooth pathway created by older generations.

In hiring relationship bankers, credit risk executives and analysts, we also placed great emphasis on technical skills and judgement. People who got through the interview stage were then asked to take a three-hour, closed-book, case-study exam that tested their financial analysis skills and their risk-management judgement. From the introduction of this test in 2017 until late 2022, the pass rate has never exceeded 47 per cent; in other words, more than half of those sitting the test, despite an otherwise impressive CV, fail to meet the required technical standards and are therefore not offered a job. While we are testing their financial mathematics in understanding the linkage and drivers between the balance sheet, profit and loss and cashflow statements of an SME business, we are also really testing their judgement. We want to understand how they think without defaulting to 'what the policy rule book says'.

One of the problems with the banking of SMEs is that the industrialisation process we described earlier has meant that far too many bankers are not skilled in core financial and risk analysis. These core capabilities have, in the name of cost reduction, been either centralised or automated. The false economy of these decisions has meant that critical thinking skills have been dramatically and concerningly weakened at the front line. As we discussed with applicants their responses to the questions in the exam, the question 'Why would you structure the transaction that way?' was often answered, 'That's what gets through the system!'

Linked to core banking skills assessment in our key hires (our senior bankers and credit executives), we look for at least 10,000 hours of credit experience (to borrow again from Malcolm Gladwell's *Outliers*). The craft of SME banking is a different competency from that of relying essentially on the collateral (security) or heavily on quantitative data (though it never ignores such data). SME banking is an experience-based capability built on the foundation of technical knowledge, one that understands how to interpret imperfect information in a way that an algorithm or credit-scoring system simply cannot. Hence, we call it a craft.

We saw the emphasis on our people as critical, from the leadership of the company to the most junior employee.

The co-CEO model

Conventional wisdom says that two heads are better than one. Two heads means double the expertise, diversity of thought and quality of decisions. It was clear to both of us that the co-CEO model was a source of competitive advantage for the company during its founding years. Co-CEO models are rare, however, and are met with deep scepticism by investors and regulators. Part of that reaction is often based on memories of organisations where two CEOs have been forced together as a function of a merger or similar situation.

Our situation, though, came from a very different background. Having worked closely together for more than ten years in different roles at two major banks, we knew each other well. We came to recognise that we complement each other with our joint values and sense of mission. So, when in 2015 we began talking about what today has become Judo, we came together around a common purpose that, in one form or other, we had been talking about for many years. We felt that if we could get the balance right and focus on our complementary skills, given our strongly aligned philosophy on the business, that one plus one would be greater than two. We enjoyed brainstorming and challenging each other, and we both appreciated that there is nothing more reassuring than knowing someone has your back, that there is someone to share highs and lows with. We both philosophically agreed with the saying, 'If you want to go fast, go alone. If you want to go far, go together'. Like all relationships, being co-CEOs required an investment in maintaining trust through constant communication. All of us have a 'shadow side' defined by strengths and weaknesses, so constantly discussing issues was something we did daily.

We were conscious of the need to make sure that the productivity or value-add of two CEOs was greater than the sum of the parts, and certainly was not dilutive in the sense of one plus one equalling one. When we look at the progress that was made in a relatively short time frame, it was in large part driven by the co-CEO model, as well as by a high-calibre leadership team. This is not to say that this model is always right for the business as it matures, nor that it is the right model for every start-up – we have seen examples where it hasn't worked – but where there is a strong philosophical alignment, a strong personal relationship, a high level of trust and a complementary set of skills and experience, the model can be a powerful one. We had all these attributes.

The potential for conflict in a co-CEO relationship is real, of course, as it is across all leadership teams given the multiple and natural pressures that arise in the early years of any business. These can relate to decisions of all types, as there will inevitably be differences of perspective and opinion; but it is also true that, on the basis that these kinds of debates are always built on the common vision, they are a natural and healthy way to progress the company. These are the best ways to deal with potential problems in the future:

- Discuss all these possibilities and a range of different scenarios upfront, and take great care in working through the principles by which you want the co-CEO model to operate at the outset and choosing the person you will share the title with.
- Stick to the maxim of having the conversations when you need to have them and in the way you need to have them.

As an absolute prerequisite, there can never be any question of the level of trust between the individuals. If there is, the model won't work, and small issues – of which there will be many – can suddenly take on larger proportions. It also means that, when the inevitable dark days come along the journey, and in whichever form they come, you know without giving it a second thought that your partner has both the company's and your interests at heart.

As we discuss in Chapter 10, in mid-2021, as we came into the IPO of the company, we both came to the view that the co-CEO model had run its natural course and it was time to revert to a more traditional model. We managed this transition in a seamless and well-planned way, and in so doing it was clear to everyone that it was a natural transition rather than an event. One of the true measures of leaders is their ability to think ahead, to get off the dancefloor of current activities and onto the balcony to reflect on the future needs of the business. Markets and businesses are always evolving, and it is important that leadership thinking does the same.

On leadership

There is an old saying in corporate governance (which is a Chinese proverb) that 'the fish rots from the head'. If the leadership of any business or function, small or large, is not leading by example, then the organisation can build a tendency to mirror that behaviour and become dysfunctional. In start-ups this can prove fatal. People can 'smell' BS or a lack of authenticity long before it is clearly visible, and it undermines everything. We vowed that no matter how talented an executive was, there would be no place for them if they were not true to the values that we had established for the bank.

Our philosophy on leadership led us to develop the 16 principles that define leadership characteristics at Judo. While we arguably developed these principles early in our evolution, we felt it important to clearly enunciate them so they acted as a reference for the leadership bench that we were seeking to build and a cornerstone of how they were evaluated. With the future very much in mind, these are the 16 principles:

1. **Be customer obsessed:** Leaders start with the customer and work backwards.
2. **Have an ownership mindset:** Leaders are owners and are personally highly accountable.
3. **Demonstrate good instincts (a lot):** Leaders have strong judgement and know when to use it.
4. **Learn and be curious:** Leaders are never done learning and always seek to improve themselves.
5. **Be resilient and mature:** Leaders keep things in perspective; they move between the dancefloor and the balcony when setting context.
6. **Think big:** Thinking small is a self-fulfilling prophecy.
7. **Hire and develop the best:** Leaders focus on our 'migrant mindset' and raise the performance bar with every hire and promotion.

8. **Insist on the highest standards:** Leaders have relentlessly high standards – many people may think these standards are unreasonably high.
9. **Bias for action:** Speed matters in business.
10. **Dive deep:** Leaders operate at all levels, stay connected to the details, audit frequently and are sceptical when metrics and anecdotes differ.
11. **Detest 'bad' bureaucracy:** Leaders avoid endless meetings, unproductive effort, long reports and poor execution.
12. **Earn trust and be aware of your 'shadow':** Leaders listen attentively, speak candidly, treat others respectfully and know that their actions speak louder than words.
13. **Know your people:** Leaders understand what motivates and drives their teams, and how to get the best from them.
14. **Have backbone, disagree and commit:** Leaders engage at 'point easy' and are obligated to respectfully challenge decisions when they disagree, even when doing so is uncomfortable or exhausting.
15. **Be committed to our values:** Leaders value trust, teamwork, accountability and performance.
16. **Foster a risk culture:** Leaders are always thinking not just about the risks in front of them but two steps ahead.

As we mention at several points in this book, different models or styles of leadership can be needed at different stages of a business's evolution. Too many entrepreneurs (like Tom Blomfield at Monzo) simply do not enjoy the administrative demands of leadership and management in a maturing business, whereas some leaders are quite adept at changing the way that they operate.

Leadership in a start-up business is very different from that in an established business. There is much evidence that leadership and management within large firms make very little difference to the performance of the organisation. This could be either because the selection process is sufficiently effective that good managers are replaced by good managers, or because managers make very little difference in some industry structures, where the power of the firm dictates outcomes regardless of the manager. Clearly the exception here is that incompetent managers can inflict much harm on the firm if unchecked. There is no equivalent in business management to the Hippocratic Oath of the medical profession in how managers should perform, and much underperformance is easily hidden by market power. Not so in a start-up: weaknesses in performance are readily visible and often fatal.

Over time as we shaped the company, there were a series of leadership competences that we consistently discussed and focused on:

- **Vision:** The leadership trait of vision is of particular importance in a start-up and growing business, and not all those in leadership positions have it. Leadership with a clear vision is essential for guiding and directing effort.
- **Influence:** Leadership is also about influencing behaviour: winning the hearts and minds of those inside the business, and generating belief in an organisation's ability to achieve stretch goals – that they can jump three metres instead of two. If they 'fail' at 2.8 metres, they have still achieved a far superior performance than achieving two metres. We learnt this philosophy on high performance from John McFarlane when he was CEO at ANZ.
- **Culture:** Leadership is about defining, refining and embedding the culture of the organisation.

- **Optimism:** No matter the external environment, leaders must be optimistic. That need for optimism was tested at the beginning of the COVID-19 crisis in 2020. At that time, Judo was a young company that found itself facing a real 'black swan' or tail-risk event. Being an optimist doesn't mean being sanguine and ignoring reality; it means holding a consistent and positive belief that we will be able to chart our way out of the crisis, and having a predisposition to see the opportunities that often emerge in a crisis.
- **Problem-solving:** Leaders must come to the table with solutions, not just problems. We occasionally used the term 'dead cat' to highlight situations when someone would metaphorically put a dead cat (problem) on the table, point at it and say, 'Look, there's a dead cat. Nothing I can do about that, it's dead'. This was a tongue-in-cheek way of calling out the importance of having spent some time thinking about what the potential solutions to the tabled problem might be, rather than simply passing it on to others to resolve.
- **Ownership:** Perhaps most importantly, leaders must take personal ownership of the culture within the business. Taking ownership of culture is tested in a crisis. We saw leaders as having the responsibility to ensure that people who actively detracted from the culture we were aspiring to embed – those that hurt the culture – were removed from the organisation. As the old saying goes: 'What you permit, you promote. What you allow, you encourage. What you condone, you own'.

The cultural tone set by the leadership team is so important. We agree with Jeff Immelt, the former CEO of GE, who said that in most leadership forums, there are four types of people:

1. Always engaged, contributing with thoughtful points and listening to other views

2. Constantly talking, drowning the meeting in detail, and not open to alternative views
3. Stays silent even though they have much to offer, and their contribution must be encouraged
4. Those who don't belong in the team, who stay silent in meetings but don't hesitate to undermine the team outside of the meeting with a contrary view.

We have had one or two people who fit the fourth type in the company, and we eventually got rid of them. The mistake we made is that we didn't remove them from the business earlier. Such individuals are huge drag on the culture of the organisation.

Remuneration

As we grew and the numbers we were recruiting from the market accelerated, we moved past our earliest developmental phases of zero or submarket remuneration, pitching our remuneration at the same level that people were being paid at the bank they were leaving to join us. We agreed in the first year to cover expected short-term incentives (STI) payments that people were leaving behind, but we made it clear that we were philosophically opposed to market-practice STI models, because we had seen the entitlement and sometimes self-serving and corrupting nature of how these work within banks. While it is very important to pay people a market rate of pay, we wanted everyone to have an equity stake and equity mindset in the business, so that they thought like owners and, if the business was successful, that the equity (a multiple of many years' aggregated STI) would make a material difference to those individuals and their families.

The design of equity ownership plans is fraught with challenges, and this is particularly the case with a start-up. It is so important to take care in how equity is allocated, and to think several steps ahead and believe three things:

1. Not everyone is going to work out, and often the needs of the business can outgrow an individual.
2. There is every likelihood that the business will need to hire key people in the future, and so allowing for this in how you think about the design and allocation of equity is critical.
3. Central to the remuneration design is trust – a fundamental and widely held belief that the process for determining and allocating remuneration is understood, transparent and appropriate.

Designing remuneration systems that anticipate these realities, is a classic case of 'measure twice, cut once'. Do not rush this, and do get expert advice. Look at innovative design in other markets, as remuneration design can be quite conventional and defined by market norms rather than creative thinking.

Remuneration design is not an exact science. It is only reasonable that early employees get the lion's share of the equity, because they took more risk; but future employees, often those with specialist skills, will be critical to the future success of the business. We have seen too many equity ownership schemes backfire, often through poor design and the tension this can create among employees when there are differences among key people or resentment towards business units (such as a poorly performing UK business unit dragging down overall business performance), leading to a fundamental and sustained lack of trust in the appropriateness and equity of remuneration. Do remember that what is intended to be a confidential agreement between the company and the employee is rarely kept a secret.

It is also not uncommon, for example, for an entrepreneur to design a scheme for key employees that starts life looking very attractive but then, through the negotiation of various rounds of new equity, is diluted away, leaving the founding owners with little to show for their efforts and risk. So, the careful design of a robust equity scheme is critical – one that clearly aligns management and founder outcomes with those of investors, and also acts as a key component of the ongoing employee proposition and in attracting talent to the company. To achieve this, the scheme should be tested, tested and retested against a whole range of scenarios. The most sceptical of risk-management lenses should be brought to bear to ensure that there are no unintended consequences. The scheme should create a genuine incentive to outperform, and align key individuals with the success of the business and outcomes for investors in a very meaningful way. Mal Hiscock and the team at Ashurst did an excellent job in designing the management incentive program (MIP). We subsequently added a long-term equity incentive scheme to cover all staff, which mirrored the main features of the MIP.

Well-structured remuneration is a hugely complex area, and so good legal advice is essential, which we were able to get from the Ashurst team. The MIP scheme provides equity allocations to participants based on a mix of time in role and the extent to which the business met its predetermined performance hurdles. Vesting rights were subject to shareholders achieving a minimum target return. (Despite our achievements in this regard, the Australian private company equity ownership rules are overly complex and, in many respects, arcane when it comes to encouraging an equity mindset in a new business. The hundred-person rule, for example, belongs to a dinosaur age.)

Culture

One of the benefits of starting a business when you are in your fifties and have led large diverse businesses is that you have a deep, intuitive and real-world understanding of the multiplicative value of a high-performing culture. We have both observed and experienced this firsthand and are believers of the saying of the great Peter Drucker that 'culture eats strategy for breakfast'.

Cultural concrete

As mentioned earlier, one of the reasons we chose the longer road of building Judo from 'a blank sheet of paper' rather than acquiring and rewiring was the unique opportunity to craft the quite distinct culture we both wanted as the company grew. We have a phrase for this within Judo: 'shaping the cultural concrete as it dries'.

To extend the metaphor, as with any new company, Judo's culture would remain 'viscous' for a time. That time, however, is finite: there is a point at which the culture 'hardens' or 'sets'. Anyone who has worked in large bureaucratic organisations where the cultural concrete dried a long time ago will be very familiar with this. That is to say that the culture is woven so inextricably into the fabric of the company that it will implacably and determinedly resist change. The substantial portion of this resistance is unconscious, in the same way that you do not have conscious control over the way your body's immune system works. The immune system within large organisations – and particularly the banks – is not to be underestimated; it is a powerful force for resisting change.

As Edgar Schein, a Professor at MIT who has written extensively and insightfully on organisational culture, wrote, 'The only thing of real importance that leaders do is to create and manage culture. If you do not manage culture, it manages you, and you may not even be aware of the extent to which this is happening'. These words are so true and potent, and such important advice is never to be ignored or forgotten.

In the Australian banking sector, exactly how this cultural concrete had set was laid bare by the Hayne Royal Commission in 2019.

The final report from the Royal Commission highlighted system-wide and deeply rooted cultural problems throughout the banking industry. We knew that if we could build 'cultural capital' within the business, it would make the difference between being a good, run-of-the-mill organisation and a great organisation.

We were also very aware that there would be challenges as we sought to shape the culture. As the business grew rapidly in employee numbers and points of representation around Australia, how would we preserve and foster the culture we wanted to define Judo? As a regulated bank, there would be practices imposed on the business that had the potential to nudge it towards aspects of the broken culture that prevailed throughout the industry. A perverse example of this to those outside the banking industry is the Banking Executive Accountability Regime (BEAR), introduced into the sector by APRA in 2020 based on a similar framework introduced in the UK. It says everything about how executive accountability had become so weak inside the industry that the regulator had to produce this prescriptive policy, which in a well-functioning industry or business would have been a normal part of governance and leadership. This issue was pointedly raised by Kenneth Hayne in the Royal Commission when he said, 'Having heard from both the CEO and the chair… I was not persuaded that NAB is willing to accept the necessary responsibility for deciding, for itself, what is the right thing to do'.

This also highlighted to us the powerful differentiation between an ownership mindset – where accountability is fundamental – and an employee mindset, where accountability can be obfuscated and fudged. The problem is that these regulations apply to all regulated banking entities, so the sins of the few are brought to bear on the many. These sins were largely a function of the culture inside the larger banks, who are advantaged in so many other ways by the oligopoly within which they operate and the regulatory rules that govern them. Such is the unintended but perverse nature of regulation.

So, consistent with our think-big philosophy, we wanted to shape our 'cultural concrete' as it dried as a multiplier of the effectiveness of our people, and so it would support the business in the future, when it would be demonstrably bigger and potentially in the public arena as a listed company. But how do you do this? The answer has nothing to do with the kind of energetic proselytising that typifies much of the cultural change work done in large corporations today; in fact, it is almost the opposite.

The first step is to define what the key 'planks' of that culture are – and, importantly, are not. The latter, in our case, was aided by the up-close view of many elements of the cultures of the major banks. The second step is to think in a real-world and practical sense about how you comprehensively weave those elements into the working fabric of the business.

As we began to define those underpinning planks, what we were effectively doing was building the culture of Judo based on the agreed values of the organisation. Very consistent with Judo's values, we framed our cultural aspirations on five key principles:

1. **Openness:** Everyone knows what is going on.
2. **Challenge:** We will challenge the status quo.
3. **Teamwork:** We respect ideas and embrace diversity.
4. **Accountability:** We are individually accountable.
5. **Owner mindset:** We want our people to think like equity owners, not 'hired hands'.

The reality inside many organisations is that they are either 'I' or 'We' in a cultural sense. 'I' organisations tend to link rewards to individual accomplishments; this works in some environments, where there is much internal competition and a high premium on individual human capital. Investment banking, the legal profession and consulting are examples of predominantly 'I' business cultures. Then there are

'We' organisations, which place greater emphasis on team cohesion and enterprise results. We wanted Judo to emphatically be a 'We' organisation from the top down. As Simon Sinek said, 'A culture is strong when people work with each other for each other. A culture is weak when people work against each other for themselves'.

In a commercial banking business, we found it difficult to understand how an 'I' culture would work. We had read Anne Boden's engaging book *Banking on It: How I disrupted an industry* and have a huge respect for what she has achieved with Starling Bank. In contrast to her view, however, we believed that the success of the business was not going to be a product of our ingenuity but of the hard work and talent of all our people, and particularly some key executives. The emphasis on 'We' was symbolically evident in the co-CEO model.

Every organisation should spend time defining the 'planks' of their own culture – ones that resonate with the purpose, values and beliefs of their enterprise. They also must find their own practical, real-world ways of embedding the drivers of culture into their operations. The key is to have a strategy for doing this.

Mental health and fitness

Building a new business can be a highly stressful endeavour, and how stress is managed can make a big difference for the business and a critical difference for the individual. We can remember days and weeks when things were looking very grim, and when sleepless nights were the norm. Of course, poor sleeping caused by stress only exaggerates the problem and leads to potential health consequences both physical and mental. In extreme situations, it is not unusual to hear of people having a complete breakdown, such as the publicised example of then Lloyds Bank CEO António Horta-Osório, who had a mental breakdown following weeks of not sleeping due to work-related stress.

Horta-Osório's willingness to publicise his condition highlighted a problem that is widespread and, unfortunately, still stigmatised in a business world where people feel reluctant to be honest and get help for a serious condition, and he deserves great credit.

Stress serves as a natural, physiological response that can help us learn, grow and achieve our goals. All of us are prone to stress in our own unique way. What causes stress in one person may seem inconsequential to others. You might remember the term 'homeostasis' from high-school biology, which is the physiological way of maintaining a stable internal environment. When we experience symptoms of stress, the homeostatic balance is affected; and to re-establish this balance, the brain triggers the release of the hormones adrenaline and cortisol into our blood. This gives us a physical energy boost and the mental focus to do what is needed – think of running from danger, or the effort to get from central London to Heathrow having just realised that you misread the time of your flight back to Sydney and you only have two hours before the flight departs, and it is peak traffic time in London! In highly stressful situations, this can cause blood flow to move away from the prefrontal cortex, the sections of the brain that are related to our higher executive functions – regulating our emotions, suppressing our biases, allowing us to think creatively and helping us solve complex problems.

We can all think of times when, under stress, our ability to think straight was compromised and we said something or acted in a way that we never would have when more composed. The problem with this natural physiological process arises when the stress response is excessive and enduring, which can ultimately trigger stress-related disease. In its early stages, chronic stress can lead to cognitive and physical burnout at work and problems at home, as illustrated in the case of António Horta-Osório.

The key is to understand your own stress temperament and how you can harness your body's normal stress response so that you are managing it, rather than being managed by it. One of the biggest problems that people have in managing their stress is their own poor self-awareness: managing stress starts with self-awareness.

There are many telltale signs of stress. As cortisol is built into the 24-hour body clock, any sleep issues – difficulty falling asleep, waking up early without feeling refreshed or even waking up in the middle of the night, together with fatigue during the day – could all be signs of high levels of cortisol. Because of the effect of cortisol to store fat around the abdomen, highly stressed individuals are also more likely to crave high sugar (including alcohol) and have high caffeine intakes to manage through periods of stress. For men in particular, the steroid effect of cortisol on fat deposition in the adipose cells around the belly can lead to unwelcome weight gain around the middle of the body. Understanding and managing stress is one of the key reasons why neuroscience is so relevant to business, and why a 'big boys don't cry' culture is not healthy. Too often, people suppress their stressful feelings; this only adds to the risk of abnormal levels of cortisol staying in the body, which can lead to physical illness, including heart attacks. We highly recommend the book *Why Zebras Don't Get Ulcers* by Professor Robert Sapolsky, on the mental and physical effects of stress, with several excellent lectures under the same heading also available on YouTube.

The connection between physical and mental health is well established. While the brain represents approximately 2 per cent of the average body's weight, it uses around 20 per cent of the body's energy. There is a seamless connection between the brain and the body, and when you are paid essentially to use your brain, it is so important to look after your body. When you compromise your physical health, it can affect your decision-making and your ability to be an effective leader.

The challenges of building a business from scratch and then managing it as it matures can impose a material mental burden on people. It was to his great credit that Tom Blomfield said on his resignation from Monzo, 'I was really struggling. I had a really, really supportive exec team around me and a really supportive set of investors on board and I was really grateful that when I put my hand up and said, "I need help", they were super receptive to that'.

Another health risk is the blurred line between someone being highly motivated, which is healthy and enriching, and addiction, which is unhealthy and damaging both to the individual and to their family. Motivation and addiction are on a spectrum; so it is in so many walks of life, including work. Many entrepreneurs and high-performing people are often closer to the 'addiction' end of the spectrum than the 'motivation' end. The ability to be resilient, mentally tough and confident, and to sustain one's self-belief, are characteristics seen in high-performing people.

The statistics on marital failure in senior businesspeople are alarming. Psychiatrists and psychologists since at least RD Laing in the 1960s have highlighted the difficulties of being both a successful family contributor (such as a father or mother) and being successful in a chosen professional field, where the individual has a burning ambition to succeed. The reality of this conflict can add considerable stress and lifetime regrets, and is therefore not a risk that someone should blindly sleepwalk into – and yet so many people do.

With these lessons in mind, we were very aware of the need to ensure a balance in managing the demands of creating and building a new business with the needs of mental and physical wellbeing. That is not to say that we always achieved a balance!

While they are no substitute for professional advice, we provide some practical tips on how to manage mental and physical wellbeing:

- **Work at maintaining balance in your life:** Even though the task of building a new business is all-consuming, some balance is essential to avoid cognitive and physical energy depletion. So, planning breaks – real breaks – is vital, as is getting off the busy dancefloor and onto the balcony to reflect and discuss. We did this regularly over lunch and dinner. It was time out. We also made sure that family time was exactly that. We followed our interests outside work, such as studying for a master's degree in psychology and neuroscience, or chairing an institute that seeks to shape the way in which future cities are designed to make them better places to live.

- **Stay connected:** When you are focused on building a business, it is so easy to neglect important relationships. This can be a big mistake. While the hours are long, we have both worked hard to make sure that we remain woven into the fabric of our friends and family. The balance and perspective this brings can't be overstated, along with the importance of allowing your brain to switch off from the challenges in the business. Many great and creative ideas come from talking to others who might bring a perspective that is fresh and valuable.
- **Do not neglect sleep:** Nearly half of the population will struggle with insomnia at some point, so this is a problem that many people have, not just entrepreneurs. In a stress-inducing world, sleep – or the lack of a quality seven to nine hours – has become a serious issue. The body and brain need sleep to replenish, and there is no way that anyone can sustain cognitive or physical effort over time without good-quality sleep. Poor-quality sleep is a sure sign of not managing stress. Often linked to poor sleep, particularly during stressful times, is the propensity to overeat and drink too much alcohol: big mistakes that form part of what can become a vicious, almost addictive cycle of trying to cope.
- **Stay hydrated:** Proper levels of hydration, together with a good diet, are critical to managing stress and cognitive prowess. Drinking two to three litres of water a day is a habit that we highly recommend.

- **Watch your diet:** As with hydration, what you eat can have a big impact on physical and mental energy levels. Poor eating habits, together with excessive alcohol levels (and sometimes other substance abuses), are linked with stress. Do not allow this to happen to you. Do not underestimate just how much a healthy gut improves your cognitive abilities. A healthy gut also impacts your level of resilience under stress.
- **Exercise:** One of the best ways to manage stress and keep the brain and body fresh is physical exercise. Too many people use the excuse of being busy and short of time for putting off an activity that could substantially improve individual performance. Frequent exercising reduces inflammation and assists in the regulation of emotions.
- **Engage in meditation, yoga or massage:** Meditation, yoga, massage and other forms of relaxation are great ways to manage stress, control anxiety, enhance self-awareness and, according to a meta-analysis of 12 studies enrolling nearly 1000 participants, it can also help reduce high blood pressure. In part, meditation appears to control blood pressure by relaxing the nerve signals that coordinate heart function, blood vessel tension and the 'fight-or-flight' response that increase alertness in stressful situations.
- **Laugh:** Laughter and a sense of fun are so important for several reasons. Laughter triggers the release of endorphins, the body's natural feel-good chemical, and helps reduce stress hormone levels. It also gets your heart pumping, so it is good for the heart. Laughing also enhances your intake of oxygen-rich air… and the list goes on. The bottom line is that laughing is good for you, and one of the great things about the co-CEO model has been that we laughed a lot over the six years we spent as co-CEOs (and we still do).

8

How to reach black belt

Ten lessons we learnt

One of the truly rewarding things about launching a new business is the learning experience. While much thought and planning went into the way that the Judo team took a PowerPoint and built a bank that is capable of being scaled, there have been many lessons along the way. Sure, we stayed true to our philosophy of 'measure twice, cut once', but as with Deng Xiaoping's pragmatic philosophy of 'crossing a river by feeling the stones', there is so much that must be reacted to in the moment. Take the approval of the banking licence, for example: that ended up taking at least six months longer than we had anticipated, and every month of delay brought with it uncertainty around capital, anxiety among the team and significant financial costs as we continued to go through our cash resources without being able to enter the lending market with any real momentum.

We have highlighted lessons throughout this book, but if we were to pick the ten key lessons on our journey, they would be as follows.

1. Vision, stamina, persistence and resilient optimism are critical

First and foremost, this is the hardest, most exciting, most nerve-racking and potentially most rewarding thing you will ever do. Nothing in business will ever be as exhilarating or compare to the feeling of living the roller-coaster that is start-up. There will be many dark days and weeks when the prospect of failure – and significant financial loss – is staring you in the face. To succeed, you need an inner strength and deeply held belief in the vision of the business that you (and others) are looking to create.

If the vision stays strong – and your resilience, persistence and stamina equally strong – then, with careful planning, excellent project management and first-class execution skills, the prospects of success are real. Johann Hari summed up the importance of this in his excellent book *Stolen Focus*: 'You need to choose one single goal; make sure your goal is meaningful to you; and push yourself to the edge of your abilities'.

If the vision fades or pivots, then so do the prospects of success. Have the Calvin Coolidge quote at the end of Chapter 6 front of mind every time you feel things are getting too hard.

With that stamina, focus and willpower, you can amaze yourself with the number and complexity of hurdles you are able to overcome. We think of that as the building of organisational muscle around problem-solving. The early days typically present big and potentially fatal challenges, but as the collective experience, intellect and creativity of the team is applied, the apparently unsolvable does get solved. By the time the 25th major hurdle presents, organisationally there is a strong level of confidence that, while answers aren't immediately clear, this challenge – as with the 24 preceding challenges – is navigable.

Being able to visualise success is so important. As Theodore Roosevelt once said, 'Believe you can and you're halfway there'.

The importance of leading a new business with an abundant mindset cannot be overemphasised.

In equal measure, it is important that a 'scarcity mindset' – the opposite of an abundant mindset – is avoided. Our brains are approximately two-and-a-half times more likely to decide to avoid loss than to seek reward (and for commercial bankers it's probably ten times), with the amygdala and hippocampus working together to present you with images and memories of all the times you have done this before and all the things that have gone wrong. It is a basic self-protection mechanism. This kind of thinking, though, particularly when you are constantly breaking new ground, can be corrosive over time and suck a huge amount of energy out of the room – the dreaded energy vampire.

Of course, to be very clear, this does not preclude the kind of constructive critique and challenge we have spoken about, nor does it obviate the need to measure twice and cut once. Rather, it speaks to embedding the key characteristics of an abundant mindset: namely, the ability to spot opportunities and to thoughtfully and confidently decision them. There is an enormous difference. As George Bernard Shaw said, 'People who say it cannot be done should not interrupt those who are doing it'.

Most importantly, an abundant mindset allows you to be personally and organisationally sustained by a resilient optimism during uncertain times. Leaders who can lead from abundance have a deep understanding of their purpose and are more able to stay the course in challenging times. Abundant leaders also think long-term and are mindful of the advice from Bill Gates that, 'Most people overestimate what they can do in one year and underestimate what they can do in ten years'. The psychological concept of willpower is important here. Willpower is the ability to delay short-term gratification to meet long-term goals. Strong willpower mitigates against the temptation to do the expedient thing, which may be gratifying in the short-term but leads to suboptimal longer-term outcomes. (Roy F Baumeister and John Tierney's *Willpower* is an excellent book on the subject.)

As important as an abundant mindset is avoiding hubris. As your young organisation grows, starts posting material successes on the scoreboard and receiving deserved plaudits, avoid the temptation to develop an organisational 'swagger'. Certainly, a quiet pride has been earned, but we have seen so many instances where the development of an overinflated corporate ego led to a complacency and sense of entitlement and, sometimes, corrupting and fraudulent behaviour. The case of WeWork under founding CEO Adam Neumann provides a classic case study (and now a highly rated TV drama: *WeCrashed*). The hubris-fuelled CEO built a business at breakneck speed, and it quickly achieved a market valuation of US$47 billion before crashing down to earth and a valuation of less than US$3 billion. The early story of WeWork provides rich insights into what can go wrong when the ego of the business founder goes unchecked through inadequate corporate governance, and financial management disciplines are lacking. As we talked about in the previous chapter, it also increases the predisposition to be attracted off the main path by new and shiny 'baubles', (as was also the case with WeWork). When it comes to corporate and individual ego, the story of Greensill Capital is hard to beat, as Duncan Mavin's book *The Pyramid of Lies* brilliantly captures.

2. Getting early decisions right is critical

Mistakes made early on can be difficult to correct, such as choosing the wrong investors, making the wrong hiring decision or selecting the wrong technology partner (a mistake we made early on). This is where our 'measure twice, cut once' philosophy was so important, and where most entrepreneurs make big and often defining mistakes. There is a temptation, with adrenaline flowing, to 'just do it', and come back and tidy up early miscalculations at a later stage. A far better saying is 'just do the work'. Like Deng Xiaoping's 'crossing the river' metaphor, Warren Buffett's saying here is instructive: 'Don't test the depth of the water with both feet'. Avoiding this risk is our strong advice.

3. Hire well to form high-functioning teams

Of all the (inevitable) mistakes made in building a new business, hiring the wrong people – particularly key personnel – is at the top of the list. This is true across business generally, but it can be particularly debilitating in the formative stages of a young company. We made this mistake. We are all susceptible to making hiring decisions based on the three R's: reputation, relationship and referrals – often without much objective rigour being applied. It is easy when you know someone to hire them. You convince yourself that much of the risk is mitigated by prior knowledge and the reputation of the individual. How many times have you known someone to flourish in one environment – perhaps because he or she had been there for decades and built strong internal networks or benefited from powerful sponsorship – and crash in a new environment? It is the same in sport. Someone can be a great player in one team and mediocre in another.

For our young business, we felt that the best way to hire was to create a more structured and objective framework based on three C's: character, competence and courage (in the context of the 'migrant mindset' we mentioned earlier). We felt that these three qualities are tailor-made for the roller-coaster journey of a new or transforming business. Conventional ways of thinking are not. Great businesses have developed a core competency in how they hire people. Many CVs are impressive, but they rarely say anything about teamwork, courage and integrity, nor do they give a good insight into the 'migrant mindset'.

Getting the right hiring practices and frameworks in place is the first step, but great businesses are rarely built by an individual: they are almost always built by a cohesive and passionate team of like-minded people. Place great emphasis on teamwork, and do rigorous due diligence to satisfy yourself that a candidate is a team player. Be sure that all key hires are fully aligned with the purpose of the business. When people are aligned with purpose, they give 100 per cent and more. If there is no alignment with purpose, effort fades over time, and you never get the best from someone. Discussions soon descend to salary and bonus levels, and the relationship becomes mercenary. As Daniel H Pink discusses in *Drive*, 'The most deeply motivated people – not to mention those who are most productive and satisfied – hitch their desires to a cause larger than themselves'.

We always reminded ourselves that people have a 'gift' they can either bring to work or not; that gift is discretionary effort, passion and motivation to go the extra mile. Never take this gift for granted, because it can be easily and quickly withdrawn.

Listen to the language applicants use: avoid the 'I's, and hire the 'We's. Again, we made this mistake, and it was time-consuming and expensive to correct. Peter Thiel describes this well in his book *Zero to One* when he talks about hiring people who can form a tribe-like passion for the business's success and who think like owners, not just 'hired hands' (a theme we return to in Chapter 9).

This leads on to collective intelligence. We have found that a highly functional team with diverse experiences and perspectives, and that is highly motivated and well facilitated, is many multiples more creative and insightful than the sum of the individual parts, and can face and solve the most complex and daunting issues. The flip side is a founder team that doesn't gel and in which conflicts arise; this can be very damaging to the business and needs to be addressed as soon as it is apparent. Make sure that the team is diverse and complementary in skills and background.

To maximise the collective challenge, a culture of robust, constructive, non-personalised challenge is essential. When that challenge is absent and it's clear there are underlying but unspoken issues, one or more individuals around the table should adopt the position of what Patrick Lencioni calls the 'miner':

> 'They must have the courage and confidence to call out sensitive issues and force team members to work through them. This requires a degree of objectivity during meetings and a commitment to staying with the conflict until it is resolved.'

GE's Jeff Immelt raised the same problem, as mentioned in earlier chapters.

Given the critical importance of hiring the right people, one of the most important hirings you will make is a first-class HR executive. This is not a luxury appointment; it will save the business a multiple of the cost of the hire.

The flip side of hiring the right people is the need to make changes in key roles as the business evolves. This can result in hardworking and passionate colleagues leaving and new hires joining, as discussed earlier.

4. Purpose and end-state vision are critical

Applying this philosophy more broadly, you cannot build a great business on flawed foundations. This is again where the philosophy of 'measure twice, cut once' becomes so important. In many ways it is a bit like the first 100 days in a new role: you never get that time again, and it is a hugely significant time in learning and mapping out how things are going to work. From presidents to prime ministers, CEOs to leaders in any organisation, the 100 days are sacred and should never be wasted. It is during this period that so many big decisions are made, and none bigger than being clear on the purpose and values of the organisation and how they are aligned with the founding leadership team. Having a strong sense of purpose that is aligned at a personal and organisational level creates the right conditions for a goal-directed and motivationally driven sense of destiny, where everyone can visualise the business that they are seeking to build. As Stephen R Covey famously said, 'Start with the end in mind'. Avoid at all costs the trap of the Cheshire cat in *Alice in Wonderland* that we mentioned in Chapter 2: 'If you don't know where you are going, any road will get you there'. So, building that vision and being able to bring it to life for everyone is a critical leadership quality that galvanises and motivates the whole organisation, and strengthens resilience, allowing people to flourish. As Martin Seligman said in his seminal book *Learned Optimism*, 'Success requires persistence, the ability to not give up in the face of failure. I believe that optimistic explanatory style is the key to persistence'.

5. Conflict is inevitable – address it early, proactively and constructively

It is 100 per cent certain that there will be conflicts in any organisation. A principle we always tried to adopt and would recommend to those building their own business is the 'point easy, point difficult, point crisis' framework illustrated in Figure 8.1.

We were introduced to this simple but powerful framework by Mickey Connolly, an author and founder of the consulting firm Conversant. This framework simply highlights the value and importance of dealing with issues head on and early, because the complexity and difficulty of dealing with those issues increases exponentially over time.

As it relates to those within the leadership and the business, conflict will also naturally arise between founders and investors and, potentially later, also between founders and boards of directors if not carefully managed. These latter conflicts often centre around ownership, control and governance. How these are managed is critical, so constant engagement with investors is vital, particularly should there be a rogue investor who seeks to influence others against what the founders of the company believe is in the best long-term interests of the company.

Regular and quality communication with investors is such an important foundation for trust and something that is all too often overlooked once the money is in the bank. Go the extra mile in making sure that investors are kept fully informed on the business. Also, stay close to those potential investors who have not yet invested: keep them abreast of progress and look on them as potential investors in the future. Again, this is something that we put a lot of energy and thought into, and we advise others to do the same. Going back to the advice that Steve Pateman at Shawbrook and Phillip Monks at Aldermore provided us in the early days, choose your shareholders carefully. We understand the temptation to take whatever money you can get, but if that money comes from a difficult investor, it can absorb huge amounts of time and energy and potentially damage the business.

Figure 8.1: Point easy, point difficult, point crisis

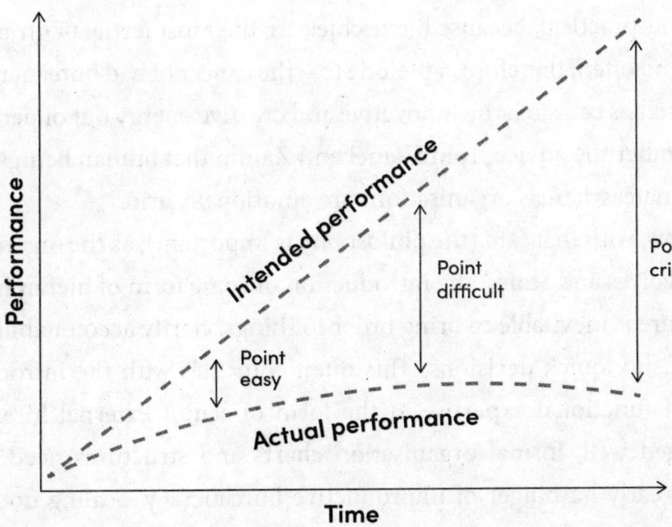

6. Keep the structure flat and take advice on the design of equity incentives

Take care in the design of remuneration, particularly when it comes to equity. It is vital to properly incentivise people for their commitment and passion; however, mistakes are often made in the initial design of equity arrangements, which are later regretted. Again, we made mistakes here and would strongly advise that good professional advice is sought on how best to design remuneration broadly, and equity rewards specifically. This again highlights the importance of having a high-calibre and experienced HR executive.

Loosely linked to remuneration is organisational design. From the outset we wanted to avoid the kind of hierarchical organisations that are endemic to big businesses the world over. In financial services this is certainly easier said than done, because it is deep in the DNA of bankers to build empires that are important symbols of power; but the rule applies across industries, particularly where you are hiring from large and incumbent organisations.

So, a strong piece of advice is to keep your organisation structures as flat as practical, because hierarchies are the most fertile of grounds for – and often, therefore, a prelude to – the cancer of bad bureaucracy. Hierarchies can suck the innovative and creative energy out of people. Remember the advice from Hamel and Zanini that human beings are passionate, whereas organisations are emotionally arid.

Now, with that said (the philosophy is important), as the organisation evolves and scales, the introduction of some form of hierarchical structure is inevitable to bring order to things, clarify accountabilities and ensure quick decisions. This often coincides with the introduction of functional expertise in the form of senior external hires. If managed well, formal organisation charts and structures need not be the early harbinger of unproductive bureaucracy. Scaling doesn't mean that a company should lose its start-up identity, as we discuss in the next chapter. The key is to anticipate and manage the growing pains of business maturity and scaling.

7. Prioritise creative thinking and the ability to deal with ambiguity

Going back to those first, seminal conversations with Joe Giannamore and Peter Cartwright at AnaCap, the wisdom of their advice to hire people who can deal with ambiguity has played out very strongly for us over time. Of course, during the hiring process everyone was asked the question, 'How comfortable are you with uncertainty, with ambiguity in your role and those around you?' Most applicants nominated themselves as strong or even thriving in that environment. The reality, though, is that many have never experienced real ambiguity, and when they have it was deeply uncomfortable for them. This is particularly the case during the first two years of a new business, which can be quite chaotic. Start-ups are not for those who like the comfort of a defined role and a clear job title, or who can't escape legacy thinking and legacy beliefs. Those things might come later, but in the early stages, it's all hands on deck.

Also, make sure that there is a good quotient of creative thinkers in the business. They are rare in business, but they are out there. Creative thinkers join dots and see patterns in a novel and thought-provoking way, and this is where breakthrough thinking can emerge. Great strategic thinkers integrate different thinking styles, seamlessly merging logical, data-driven thinking with strong intuition. They understand the importance of emotional intelligence and culture, and can pepper in intuition, bringing these and other thinking qualities to life in quite a unique way. This contrasts with those who think in a heavily analytical and logical manner: there's nothing necessarily wrong with this style – it defines most people – but it can result in *good* outcomes as distinct from *great* outcomes, solid B's but not A's. We augmented our internal capabilities with some external help, particularly through a great friend of Judo, Vimpi Juneja. Armed with an MBA from Harvard Business School, Vimpi was a strong and provocative but always constructive strategic thinker who was also blessed with a great sense of humour. His ability to see patterns and challenge conventional thinking while getting his views across with humour greatly shaped how we thought about the business, not just at the outset but throughout the journey of growing the business. He highlighted the importance of doing something that you enjoy doing, and how that is so much more powerful than any other motivation. At a young age of 52 years, Vimpi unexpectedly left this world in 2021. He is greatly missed, and he will never be forgotten for his contribution to Judo's development and for his friendship.

8. Constantly seek to shape the culture

Think about culture at a macro level and at a micro level. At the macro level, be very clear on the culture that you are seeking to build. Culture can be the defining factor of a business's success and a huge multiplier of its potential. As we discussed in earlier chapters, early-stage organisations have the unique opportunity to shape the 'cultural concrete' of the organisation as it dries. At the micro level, think long and hard about how, in a practical way, you embed the cultural drivers throughout the company of the way things are done, from the big to the small. Keep in mind this Peter Thiel quote: 'Every company doesn't have a culture; every company is a culture'. The truth is that if you are not shaping the organisation's culture, it is shaping the organisation and will define your success.

It's what people do and how they behave in all kinds of situations that defines and, over time, cements an organisational culture. At the sharp end of this, it is of paramount importance that the leadership team live the culture, that they are conscious in all situations of the energy they are bringing to the situation (or, indeed, sucking out of it). Leaders are the definitive role models, and the way they behave is often consciously and, in many cases, unconsciously mirrored throughout the company.

Allowing the metaphorical concrete to dry in a random or unplanned way, or with flaws in it, just sets you up for significant and increasingly intractable problems later. There is no way a business can achieve its potential if its cultural makeup is weak, and cultural problems will most definitely weaken strategic intent. Cultural atrophy can also happen easily: it only takes one or two people who are misaligned with the purpose and values of the organisation in a way that is visible to many, and your problems can start to take root. Once those roots dig deep, then dysfunctional teams will soon follow.

All businesses would love a culture where people cannot wait to get to work and are strongly aligned to the purpose of the business. Wherever you see behaviour that is contrary to the culture you are seeking to build, move on the source of the problem and act.

We come back to the centrality of culture in the next chapter (when we discuss 'founder centrism'), because the challenges of developing culture as a business scales should never be underestimated. The 'old guard' nostalgically remember the early days, and the 'new guard' see all that is wrong with the business. A lot of start-ups struggle to develop the culture that made the place so exciting in the early days and fail to take steps to codify and reinforce important cultural values.

9. Choose your partners, including third-party suppliers, very carefully

We have always sought to build real partnerships with our key providers, and have always valued and built a particularly strong sense of loyalty to those who supported us in our early days. We have found that, when your key partners are more than simply in a transactional relationship but are metaphorically 'inside the tent' with you, there is a depth of understanding they bring that can create material value. As with the customer relationships that are central to Judo, these relationships grow over time. Reference-checking must be a central element of that third-party-vendor selection process – and not just the references provided, but those that aren't. We made a mistake here that cost us several months of momentum and millions of dollars in direct costs. This is particularly the case with critical IT providers.

10. Watch out for bureaucracy

Bureaucracy can spread like a virus, and this is particularly the case as the business grows. There's a quote broadly attributed to Oscar Wilde that summarises this: 'A bureaucracy expands to meet the needs of an expanding bureaucracy'.

The paradox of growth is that it can beget complexity – and, with it, bureaucracy, which in turn can kill growth. The illustrations in Chapter 9 summarise what can happen as businesses grow and when the founder mindset is lost: over time, the business takes on many of the cultural traits of the large incumbents. Ultimately the advantages of being a founder-led start-up are lost, and the characteristics of the incumbents begin to define the culture and operations of the business. We called this the 'mini-me' risk.

Bureaucracy and culture go hand in hand. Hamel and Zanini summed up the bureaucracy problem perfectly when they wrote:

> 'In a bureaucracy, megawatts of emotional energy get wasted on petty battles, data gets weaponized against adversaries, collegiality gets shredded by zero-sum promotion tournaments, and decisions get corrupted by artfully concealed self-interest.'

Perhaps somewhat dramatically, we can underscore the threat of bureaucracy with a great quote from Boutros Boutros-Ghali, a former Secretary-General of the United Nations, who said, 'The lesson I learned in Cairo still applies. The only way to deal with bureaucrats is with stealth and sudden violence'.

Reflection on other things we learnt along the way

Our experience of building Judo Bank during COVID-19, and as 50-plus entrepreneurs, also provided us with some further insights worth sharing.

COVID-19

Building a new bank in the 'eye of the COVID-19 storm' was not easy. It added hugely to the capital-raising challenge, with many investors understandably concerned about customer loan defaults. However, COVID-19 offered many insights into people and businesses (as well as politicians!). All private-sector businesses, to a greater or lesser extent, have been impacted by the pandemic that engulfed the world. The resilience of many people and businesses was tested in a real crisis-management sense. A positive, however, was the way that the pandemic has turbocharged many businesses' adoption of digitalisation, automation and AI. Millions of workers in the so-called 'knowledge economy' now have greater flexibility around how and where they organise their work. On Census Day 2016, 4 per cent of Australians worked from home – some 430,000 people. In a post-COVID-19 world, that figure may climb above 20 per cent, if not higher. We see this as a positive development because of the greater flexibility it allows individuals.

However, making remote working work for both the individual and the business is not something that we take for granted. Not all employees have the luxury of a home office: many live in small living areas, sometimes sharing with housemates and sometimes with small children who need to be entertained. Equally, spending your day on back-to-back Zoom calls is not for everyone: it can be draining, and most people feel Zoom fatigue after a while. We are social animals, and most of us thrive on social interaction. For this reason, the office environment will always be important. It is more than a place to work, and it must be a place where people feel safe and happy to congregate, cooperate, innovate, problem-solve, learn, socialise and celebrate.

Ageism

It should come as no surprise that we have something to say about how society treats age. As a society, we are rightly fixated on the prevalence of sexism and racism, but less so on another form of discrimination: ageism. While ageism works both ways, with discrimination existing against those considered 'too young' as well as 'too old', our focus is on the latter. As an ABC article commented, 'Being 50-plus in the workplace in Australia in 2022 is like being gay in the 1970s… it's something you can't be open about if you want to get a job and keep it'. Yet, given demographic trends, we are living longer, with forecasts indicating that 25 per cent of workers in Australia, the UK and the USA will be over 55 by 2025. People 60 and older are projected to soon outnumber children under five in most developed economies. The over-65s group in the OECD is set to increase to 25 per cent of the population by 2050.

Despite these trends, and despite what the law has to say on it, ageism is rampant in business and other aspects of life in Australia. In the 2021 report *What's Age Got to Do with It?*, Kay Patterson, Australia's Age Discrimination Commissioner, wrote, 'Ageism is arguably the least understood form of discriminatory prejudice. Evidence also suggests it is more pervasive and socially accepted than either sexism or racism'.

Age discrimination in both retention and hiring presents an invisible hurdle to keeping otherwise talented and valuable people in the workforce for longer. Most companies – more than two-thirds of those interviewed in one study – view age as a competitive disadvantage, because older workers are perceived as more expensive, less adaptable, less energetic and less able to handle the pace of digitalisation. In the knowledge economy, much of this is confirmatory bias and not supported by scientific evidence. What the science shows is that people can continue to grow mentally through the power of neuroplasticity, and that older people can have greater knowledge and experience in aspects of the business. Older employees also add to the diversity of the organisation and are great mentors to younger employees.

There is a special category of older worker – a category that we both fall into – which is those who have held high-powered corporate roles and then decided to enter a new career chapter. We know many senior executives who have struggled with the transition from high-powered roles into something else. This transition can be a hugely positive recalibration – finding that without the metaphorical 'stripes on your arm', your jokes aren't quite as funny, and your calls don't get returned with the same speed or interest. The transition involves redefining yourself and coming to terms with the reality that the trappings and privileges of a senior corporate role are no longer available and are devoid of any real meaning anyway. Far too many people have allowed their self-identity to be defined by their corporate status, and many have become addicted to the trappings of power. Senior executive roles provide individuals with a lot more than an income: they provide a structure to life and open networks and friendships that otherwise might not be available.

The sad reality, also, is that many senior executives sacrifice or neglect many other parts of their life in pursuit of corporate success and can lose touch with the realities of life. The addictive nature of high-powered jobs often means that little thought or planning is put into life after the job, and the withdrawal symptoms can be difficult to manage. Moving from a powerful role into a non-executive or not-for-profit role is major change and, for some, not easily navigated.

For these reasons, planning what your post-corporate life should be is important, and starting your own business is one serious option for many.

We believe in the power of diversity, and we included age diversity in our measure of diversity more broadly and made sure that, as with other forms of discrimination, our older employees were made to feel as valuable as any other employee. The problem is that we have a societal paradigm around old age that is based on when our grandparents were around, and is thus understandable to a point because we formed this view at a relatively young age and it became encoded. The reality, of course, is that most older people today are not inactive, lacking cognitive reasoning or sick. As *The Economist* argued, 'a radically different approach to ageing and life after 65 is needed… The average 65-year-old in the rich world can now expect to live for another 20 years'.

The silver lining in what is an otherwise disappointing reflection of modern society – as all discrimination is – is that fact that many 'older' workers who are let go, or who decide that they no longer fit, go on to start new businesses and never look back. In the USA, those between the ages of 55 and 65 are now more likely to start up new businesses than those between 20 and 34, and the success of those businesses counters the age-old myth that older people are necessarily less inventive, entrepreneurial and productive than their younger counterparts.

There is no doubt that, as people age, that there is some deterioration in some cognitive functions, such as recalling names and other details. The brain can shrink up to 5 per cent per decade after the age of 40, and areas important for memory and cognition, such as the hippocampus and prefrontal cortex, are often most affected. It is a neuroscience myth that the best way to combat these problems is by doing crosswords and sudoku, whereas there is growing neuroscience research suggesting that physical activity improves the chances of maintaining executive functions, together with a healthy diet. Naturally this varies considerably by individual, and we all know people in their late 80s or 90s with sharp minds, so generalisations are part of the discriminatory process. Neuroscientists now know that cognitive abilities don't simply level off in middle age and then start to gradually decline. Instead, the brain is continuously changing and developing across our lives. Sure, some cognitive functions can weaken, but others can improve.

Offsetting some of the potential downsides of aging is the fact that older people have a lifetime of accumulated knowledge and experience, and can have rich insights into what can go wrong with a particular course of action or strategy and the several alternative ways they've seen to attack the same problem over their career. How many times have people made mistakes that a more experienced hand would have cautioned against, or at least helped map out the risks involved so they could be managed? If you are starting up a new business, having access to experience is a critical success factor in most cases.

9

The challenger mindset

Maintaining founder centrism

As the business grew, there was a progressive realisation of how challenging it would be to maintain that special sense of ownership or founder centrism that had been so critical to Judo Bank's early success. We had many deep discussions as we defined the challenge we were going to progressively face, including around whether we had the right team in place for the next phase of the business.

The academic research on how businesses change as they scale is very persuasive about the fact that few members of an initial team of founders are likely to successfully migrate from being a 'jack-of-all-trades' start-up entrepreneur to a manager in a larger, more structured organisation. Research is also consistent on how start-up leadership teams can change several times before the business reaches scale, paralleling the advice given to us by Joe Giannamore very early on. This was a concern for us, because we believed strongly, passionately, that a founder mindset is a source of competitive advantage that must not be allowed to fade. A founder mindset was also an important anchor and definer of our culture, something that made Judo quintessentially different from others in an industry where differentiation beyond brand logos was difficult to discern.

Research has shown that by the time a start-up is three years old, some 50 per cent of founder CEOs have moved on, and fewer than 25 per cent lead their companies to a public listing. In his book *Why Startups Fail*, Thomas Eisenmann highlights research that shows 61 per cent of start-up CEOs are no longer in that role by the time of the fourth capital raise. These are sobering statistics, particularly since most founder CEOs don't go voluntarily: instead, investors through the board insist that they relinquish control, often to outsiders who don't have that special context or emotional connection with the business.

Whereas we began working on the move to a single-CEO model roughly 12 months before our IPO (and did so with the blessing of our investors), as we outline in Chapter 10 on taking Judo public, for most founder CEOs and senior founding executives it comes as a shock when they are encouraged to move on. This is often no matter how large the financial payoff might be. Many founders believe that only *they* can make the business successful and, at a personal level, they relate to the business as if it was part of their identity, almost 'part of the family'. (Some founders think of the business as 'their baby'.) A founder CEO's emotional strengths can quickly become their and the company's greatest liability, something we have seen both in Australia and overseas.

The first indication that things are changing is in the formation of the board. A board is a clear sign that the focus is moving from building a business to building an organisation. The building of the organisation requires more resources and structure and a whole range of new skills embodied in professional management. The wise founder team are proactive and stay ahead of this inevitable development by starting to build the team and strengthen the organisation themselves. This is important both in evolving the organisation and protecting its culture, because the wrong appointment into the senior ranks of a young company can be detrimental for all the reasons spelt out in lessons two and three in the previous chapter.

The second reality is the move from a jack-of-all-trades management philosophy to a more structured system of formal organisational design, job descriptions, employee performance routines and structures, and the appointment of specialist experts into key roles, who in turn often bring their friends from previous employers. As Thomas Eisenmann notes, as start-ups scale, staff, structures and shared values all undergo significant transition, which needs very careful and skilful management. The early employees of a start-up are normally highly motivated by a sense of mission and camaraderie. They feel special; they feel like pioneers and 'owners'. Things can change as the company matures and new people join the business. Sometimes, if not managed well, the culture in the organisation can start to come under strain. There is a risk of 'camps' or silos forming with 'the original employees' and 'the new employees' – the 'old guard' and the 'new guard'. This can be particularly evident when senior professional hires come in and start to dismantle what has gone before, sometimes without regard to the context in which early decisions were made. Equally, later-stage hires might be resentful of the wealth that early employees have amassed through equity interests.

In this transition to more professional management, there is an inherent 'founder's dilemma', as Noam Wasserman called it, between holding onto control (power), optimising the potential of the business and maximising personal wealth. Most founder CEOs want all three, but few can have this outcome. At a certain point in an organisation's evolution, different skills are often needed, as we discussed in Chapter 3. A founder CEO motivated by control will consider it a failure when asked to step aside, whereas if the motivation is personal wealth – or, as in our case, creating a simpler and more intuitive structure in the best interests of the company running into an IPO – then the decision to bring in a new candidate as CEO (or move to a single-CEO model, as we did) will be viewed as a thoughtful and rational move. When the founder CEO's succession is handled well, it can be in the organisation's interest to retain them on the board. This is quite common and, among other things, ensures that the founder's link is strengthened at the board level and not lost to the business. Such a move can also be prudent risk management by the board, because not only will there be a board member with deep knowledge of the business and its history, but there will also be an emergency option for the board if the new CEO doesn't work out for whatever reason.

The whole question of CEO succession should always be front of mind for a board and for founder CEOs. The literature is extensive on this. The data shows that most CEOs – approximately 80 per cent – are appointed because of an internal promotion. We believe this to be critical if a founder-centric culture is to prevail. Given the criticality of CEO appointments, we believe it is important that boards play an active role in understanding talent development within a business, and personally get to know key executives and emerging talent.

As an organisation evolves, with most of the original founders leaving the leadership team and new executives joining, the challenge of maintaining a 'founder mindset' is critical to the future of the company and is not to be underestimated. As we were preparing for an IPO, investors regularly highlighted their bias for a strong 'founder mindset' in businesses they invest in. The statistics on founder-led companies' performance compared to traditional 'hired management'-led companies provide compelling evidence of the power of the former, as we explore in this chapter.

The power of a founder mindset

The economic theory underpinning founder centrism is best understood through the principal–agent problem, which dates back to at least 1776 when Adam Smith wrote in *An Inquiry into the Nature and Causes of the Wealth of Nations*:

> 'The directors… being the managers rather of other people's money than of their own, it cannot well be expected that they should watch over it with the same anxious vigilance with which the partners in a private copartnery frequently watch over their own… Negligence and profusion, therefore, must always prevail, more or less, in the management of the affairs of such a company.'

Adam Smith and Karl Marx did not agree on much, but they both thought that the corporate form, where directors owned very little of the firm they were stewards of, was unworkable for remarkably similar reasons.

While modern corporate governance addresses some of the issues inherent in the principal–agent problem, it only scratches the surface. All the evidence supports the theory that businesses materially owned (in a personal sense) by those who manage its affairs outperform firms where the managers and directors have little personal wealth at risk. This is the core of founder centrism and is clearly illustrated by Figure 9.1.

Figure 9.1: Founder-led companies outperform the rest

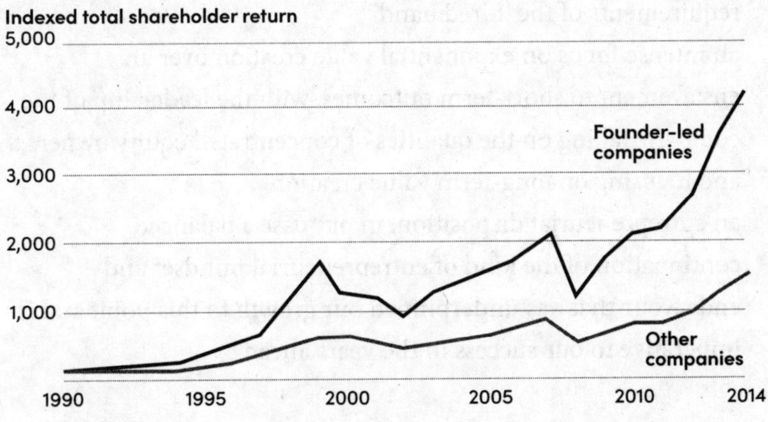

SOURCE: BAIN & COMPANY © HBR.ORG

The investment bank Credit Suisse provided more detailed insight in their analysis of the best performing ASX companies over the past 30 years (as shown in Table 9.1), revealing a common theme: nearly all these companies are either founder-led or have been led by the same CEO for a very long time – that is, much longer than the average CEO tenure of five years.

According to Credit Suisse, backing founder-led companies is compelling. This perspective is, of course, consistent with the principal–agent problem, and with the numerous other studies that have universally shown management teams with a founder-centrism mindset outperform the hired-hands mindset that prevails in most public companies. In contrast to founder-mindset management teams, hired-hands management cultures are often characterised by short-termism, internal politics, silo-based outcomes and personal brand motives overriding the interests of the enterprise and long-term value creation.

The concept of founder centrism is based on the idea that the leaders in the business have a founder's mindset, which involves:

- a deeply personal sense of the importance of the performance and success of the company, far greater than the utilitarian requirements of the 'hired hand'
- an intense focus on exponential value creation over an enslavement to short-term outcomes, with the leadership of the company taking on the qualities of concentrated equity owners and focusing on long-term value creation
- an entrepreneurial disposition, in our case a balanced continuation of the kind of entrepreneurial mindset and endeavour that has underpinned our growth to this point and is imperative to our success in the years ahead.

Table 9.1: The best-performing ASX companies over the past 30 years

Rank	Company	IPO date	Total return	Total return annualised	Leadership
1	Dicker Data Ltd	24/01/2011	19,729%	65%	Founder led
2	Fortescue Metals Group Ltd	20/03/1987	4,531,723%	43%	Founder led
3	Mineral Resources Ltd	27/07/2006	14,750%	39%	Founder led
4	Audio Pixels Holdings Ltd	23/12/2004	13,990%	35%	Founder led
5	Domino's Pizza Enterprises Ltd	13/05/2005	10,087%	33%	Founder led
6	Corporate Travel Management Ltd	15/12/2010	1960%	33%	Founder led
7	Chalice Mining Ltd	23/03/2006	6473%	32%	Founder led
8	ARB Corp Ltd	26/06/1987	319,351%	31%	Founder led
9	Magellan Financial Group Ltd	01/07/2004	9202%	30%	Founder led
10	Orocobre Ltd	03/12/2007	3553%	30%	Founder led
11	Australian Ethical Investment	16/12/2002	13,231%	30%	Founder led
12	Northern Star Resources Ltd	16/12/2003	8,835%	29%	Founder led
13	Monadelphous Group Ltd	30/04/1986	152,677%	28%	Founder led
14	Sonic Healthcare Ltd	29/05/1987	150,260%	28%	Founder led
15	Credit Corp Group Ltd	01/09/2000	16,333%	28%	CEO for last 13 years

Rank	Company	IPO date	Total return	Total return annualised	Leadership
16	McMillan Shakespeare Ltd	12/03/2004	6777%	28%	Founder led
17	MNF Group Ltd	17/05/2006	3953%	27%	Founder led
18	CSL Ltd	30/05/1994	65,579%	27%	CEO for last 8 years
19	nib Holdings Ltd/Australia	02/11/2007	2373%	26%	Founder led
20	REA Group Ltd	01/12/1999	15,575%	26%	
21	Atlas Arteria Ltd	25/01/2010	1306%	26%	
22	JB Hi-Fi Ltd	23/10/2003	5692%	26%	Last 2 CEOs had long tenure
23	Sandfire Resources Ltd	03/03/2004	4869%	25%	Founder led
24	Codan Ltd/Australia	26/11/2003	5194%	25%	CEO for last 11 years
25	Pro Medicus Ltd	09/10/2000	10,255%	25%	Founder led
26	IGO Ltd	16/01/2002	7626%	25%	CEO for last 7 years
27	Breville Group Ltd	25/05/1999	13,502%	25%	
28	Nick Scali Ltd	25/05/2004	4110%	24%	Founder led
29	Data#3 Ltd	23/12/1997	15,388%	24%	Founder led
30	AUB Group Ltd	15/11/2005	2663%	23%	

SOURCE: CREDIT SUISSE

We were committed to maintaining a strong founder-mindset culture within the leadership of Judo. Central to a 'founder centrism' model is the importance of having a board that understands and supports this mindset, which is not the norm in a public company. Conversely – and as is common in most public companies – one of the most potent forces to undermine that mindset is a board and governance regime whose actions are more akin to those of hired management, placing greater emphasis on 'independence' and 'compliance' than on entrepreneurialism and long-term value creation. This is a common problem in modern corporate governance, and even more so in regulated institutions. The concern is that, in extremis, an overly conservative board can weaken the founder spirit and, over time, create a governance model that may undermine long-term success – ironically and perversely creating an inverse set of agency costs. We were lucky that the Judo board understood how to strike the right and appropriate balance.

In Chris Zook and James Allen's excellent book *The Founder's Mentality*, they highlight that most companies that achieve sustainable growth have a set of motivating ideas in common that can be traced back to the bold vision that launched or fundamentally transformed the company. Such companies retain their 'challenger' mindset, as Zook and Allen note, 'waging war on their industry and its standards on behalf of an underserved customer'. Such companies are driven by a clear sense of purpose, and everyone inside the company knows exactly what it stands for. (You would struggle to find many staff inside large organisations that share a common understanding of their employer's purpose.) Companies that have this kind of culture tap into a deep vein of employee engagement and alignment. People inside the company feel like more than just 'hired hands'; they feel like owners and builders of a business rather than 'cogs in a wheel'.

Zook and Allen break down the drivers of that founder mentality under three key headings:

1. **Insurgency:** having a bold mission; a constant emphasis on competitive differentiation; a limitless horizon
2. **A frontline obsession:** relentless experimentation; frontline empowerment; customer advocacy
3. **An ownership mindset:** a strong cost focus; a bias to action; an aversion to bureaucracy.

All too often, however, companies lose their founder-mindset culture as they become larger and more complex. This was the challenge that we knew we had to face. We knew we wanted to maintain the all-important sense of being a founder-led company as we scaled the business. This became our central focus: how to develop and deeply embed not an 'employee' mindset but an 'owner' mindset. We believed strongly that, if this was successfully nurtured and invested in, it would become a powerful determinant of the culture we want Judo to be defined by. Being a larger bank in the future need not result in a loss of our founder spirit and the three headline drivers described by Zook and Allen.

We were encouraged by research published by the University of Oxford showing how the leadership at JPMorgan Chase & Co under CEO Jamie Dimon had developed a culture of founder centrism, even though JPMorgan Chase & Co is a big institution with a long history and widely held ownership. To some degree, we had seen the emergence of founder centrism at ANZ under the stewardship of John McFarlane, who led by example from 1998 to 2008, when he invested all his salary (except for $44 to pay for his membership of the bank's social club) in the bank's equity. These types of leaders inside large corporations are very rare: most CEOs take comfort from their substantial salaries as protection from the risks of being exposed to the equity in the businesses that they run. It is no surprise to us, then, that founder-centric companies outperform conventionally owned public companies.

A founder-centric brain is wired and works differently compared to that of most other people, argues Tara Swart et al in *The Neuroscience for Leadership*. Peter T Bryant and Elena Ortiz Terán also convincingly argue this in a 2013 *Harvard Business Review* article entitled 'Entrepreneurs' Brains are Wired Differently'. In a classic neuropsychological Stroop test (which assesses the ability to inhibit cognitive interference that occurs when processing specific stimuli) of 30 founder entrepreneurs and 30 non-entrepreneurs, scanning techniques to measure brain activity showed that the brain activity of the founder entrepreneurs was significantly different to that of the non-entrepreneurs. Founder entrepreneurs were quicker to respond to problems and less inhibited. They quickly absorbed and embraced problems despite their ambiguity. They dedicated more brain resources to resolve residual ambiguities. This quickness of response without compromising the quality of their analysis was a defining difference in the favour of the founder entrepreneur.

The paradox of growth

Chris Zook and James Allen talk through what they describe (and we totally agree) as the 'paradox of growth'. As a business grows in scale and complexity, this increased complexity 'kills' growth. Complexity brings with it bureaucracy, which stifles creativity and innovation and, consequently, a high-performance culture. The good news, as Zook and Allen confirm, is that this potential crisis is both predictable and preventable.

What we call a 'challenger' Zook and Allen call an 'insurgent'. (We liked the provocative sense associated with that label but felt that it had some negative connotations in a politically correct world.) The key insight and message revolves around navigating the complexities of growth, particularly in a heavily regulated banking business. How can we grow to achieve our scale objectives while maintaining the vitality, agility, passion and speed of a challenger – the traits that made the business so successful in its formative years?

The first thing we had to do was make sure that everyone working in the business had an equity stake in the company. This was very important to us. Even though some of the equity stakes may have at first looked modest to some people, we wanted everyone to think about how much their equity might be worth in the future if we all succeeded in building a great bank. The second important thing we had to do was make sure people understood how equity ownership, founder centrism and our challenger status were all fundamentally interlinked and self-reinforcing. We wanted people to have that 'migrant mindset' that we described earlier, to be as hungry and ambitious as a challenger must be to succeed, and to believe in the aforementioned 'David and Goliath' parable.

'Mini-me' trap

As we talked about when referring to shaping the 'cultural concrete' as it dries, we believed that there was no natural reason why the founder mindset should fade over time, even when we and other co-founders moved on. We also knew, though, that we had to proactively manage this and think of it as a cultural issue at its core rather than one of policies, procedures, systems and governance. A critical component of maintaining the founder mindset was to ensure that we were customer obsessed: that we thought about the customer in everything that we did, and that we avoided the bureaucratic traps we have discussed in many parts of this book. We knew that, unless we proactively managed and cultivated a founder-centric culture, we would naturally sleepwalk into becoming a 'mini-me' version of the incumbents.

Figure 9.2 shows how the 'mini-me' trap works. The challenger (or insurgent) starts life in the bottom-right quadrant (high benefits of founder mentality, low benefits from scale and scope), and as it achieves scale it may drift into the part of the map occupied by the incumbents (low benefits of founder mentality, high benefits from scale and scope). In banking, the regulator is a major force in this happening, and boards of directors can be, too. This is where Zook and Allen's paradox of growth kicks in: the addition of bureaucratic rituals and routines, sometimes with the addition of new senior external hires, adds to a powerful force of internal change that drives complexity and its first cousin, bureaucracy. In aggregate, these forces weaken and can eventually push out the founder mindset. These problems don't emerge out of the blue, but rather are like high blood pressure: they build up over time and can be a 'silent killer'.

Figure 9.2: The 'mini-me' trap

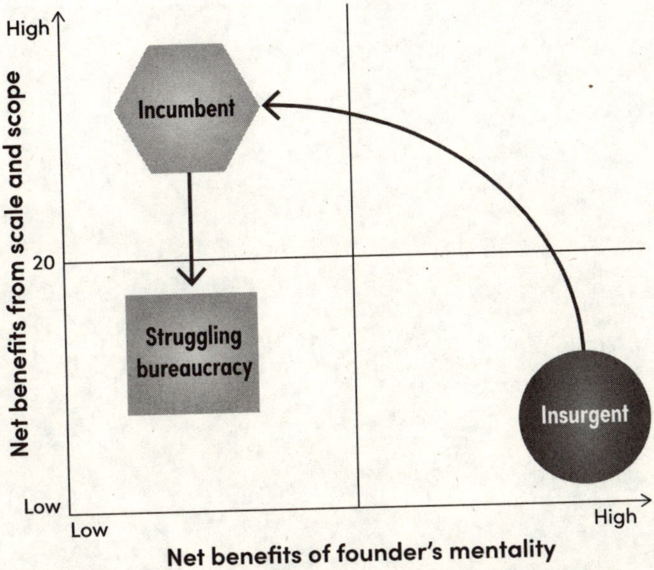

SOURCE: VIDEO FOUNDER'S MENTALITY® AND THE PATHS TO SUSTAINABLE GROWTH BAIN & CO

If these problems are not managed early and proactively before the signs of the 'disease' are visible, it is very difficult to address them at a later stage. Slowly but surely, the organisation will be bogged down in bad bureaucracy, and the end will have begun as the business drifts into the dreaded bottom-left quadrant (low benefits of founder mentality, low benefits from scale and scope). The founder mindset – as defined by the three key headings outlined by Zook and Allen – is weakened and ultimately conquered by the cancer of bureaucracy. This is a real risk to the inner health of the organisation and highlights the importance of not taking the cultural capital of the organisation for granted. A founder-centric culture is a powerful source of differentiation and a driver of superior performance; protect it and invest in it, or a 'mini-me' destiny is inevitable, and what might have made the business special in its early years will be lost, never to be rediscovered.

10

Sharing our start-up with the world

Taking Judo public

While the private capital markets had been incredibly supportive of Judo, and we had built a strong working relationship with our investors – many of whom had been with us from the first capital raise in 2017 and 2018 – we reluctantly formed the view that, with the strong growth and momentum of the company, we needed to further bolster the capital foundation of the business to underpin its next growth horizon. Therefore, it was in the best interests of the company to consider a public market listing. The motivation for going public is important: our decision was not motivated by the desire for an 'exit event', but rather was a response to how we saw the business growing and an acknowledgement of the greater certainty of accessing capital in the public market. As a bank, relying on private markets added complexity because of the 20 per cent limit placed on the amount of equity that can be held by individual shareholders. As we were raising more equity to fund growth, this cap had the potential to create problems given that we had already raised $1.2 billion of equity.

This decision to go public was a considered one, because we had always contemplated that such an event would be for 2023–24. Also, several new complexities and challenges would come from being a rapidly growing bank in a listed environment, not least of which was the question of how investors would value a unique, pure-play SME bank in a market where there hadn't been a listing of a new commercial bank for over 25 years.

The first of those new challenges would be the unique set of shorter-term performance pressures in what is one of the most overanalysed sectors anywhere in the world: the Australian banking sector. Moving from a group of private institutional shareholders who we knew well, and who knew us well, to a more dispersed register of new shareholders we felt could change the dynamic and potentially result in a shorter-term focus, rather than being in the longer-term interests of the company. You may recall that we described this as one of the cornerstones of founder centrism in the previous chapter.

Secondly, in a public equity environment, the expectations of that broader base of new investors can often be framed by benchmarking to the industry incumbents, which can be less relevant than to more analogous peers. Given the rate of Judo's growth in an industry that is largely ex-growth, this was always going to be a challenge. Ideally, young businesses should stay in the private arena for as long as possible and not be distracted by the demands of being public. Too many young companies rush to the public market when more patience and more emphasis on building the organisation would produce a much better outcome. A related challenge is the fixation of the public market on dividends, if not in the early years then in the foreseeable future. Also, essentially putting your company in play means that you can lose control of your destiny.

With the company's interest guiding our decision-making, we went to the board in late 2020 with a recommendation that we should pursue a public listing and appoint an advisor to assist us in the journey. We realised this was not a journey that should be undertaken lightly: it not only represented a significant milestone for the company but had the potential to change the way that the company was managed – and, if not handled and managed well, the very essence of our founder-centric culture. As discussed earlier, we recognised that the co-CEO model, which had been an integral part of our success, was not a management model that the public market generally welcomes; so, as an integral part of our thinking towards a move to the public markets, we began planning the move to a single-CEO model, once again putting the interests of the company first.

We also felt we needed a leadership team that was committed to the company for the next five years, and some of our co-founders, who had contributed so much to the success of the business, informed us that they just weren't able to make that commitment. Given the huge degree of heavy lifting that had been done in the previous four years, this is something we had anticipated, and our deep thinking on the make-up of the skills we needed in place for Judo's next horizon meant that we were well prepared in our thinking on succession planning, including the introduction of key executives from outside the business.

Appointing capable advisors is critical to any IPO. We appointed Barrenjoey, Citibank, Credit Suisse and Goldman Sachs to advise us on the process and help position the company within the public equity market. We were lucky that we had a very capable and experienced executive in Andrew Leslie inside the company to manage the process, both internally and in coordinating the activities of our advisors. In addition to the investment bank advisors, we had Ashurst (led by Stuart Dullard) expertly lead the due diligence committee (DDC). Our auditors, PwC, also played an important role. High-quality advisors are not only a source of market intelligence, but they also play a key role in ensuring that the important disclosures that a company makes are verified and supported by evidence and facts. They also help navigate the important requirements of regulators and the law.

IPOs are not only a huge, six-month-plus distraction for management from operational activities – you can't put the business on hold – but the time involved in investor meetings, non-deal roadshows (NDRs), cornerstone investor meetings, retail investor meetings and so on is a heavy commitment and represents only a fraction of the effort required inside the company in getting 'IPO ready'. Huge demands are placed on the company secretariat, legal, marketing and people and culture teams, to name only a few of the functions embroiled in what is a herculean undertaking. Great demands are also placed on the time of directors, with literally thousands of very detailed pages of documents to review and a materially increased board and DDC schedule making large demands on their time.

They are also expensive: depending on the size of the issue, completing a successful IPO can cost upward of $40 million for a mid-sized business. Equally, though, so much must go right to ensure a successful IPO; and for that reason alone, having a deeply experienced team of advisors and lead managers around you to navigate what is a hugely complex and nuanced process means that it is money well spent. This is not a time to 'nickel and dime': the stakes are too high, and reputations and brands can be damaged if things don't go well.

The successful completion of the IPO represents an important milestone, but it is only the beginning of new chapter, and it brings a whole new set of challenges and responsibilities. As a public company, the affairs of the business are transparent and visible to the market. Public companies are obligated to keep the market informed on all material matters, and the business is subject to a greater degree of scrutiny. The valuation of the company is also subject to market determination, and this is not something – as we found out during the difficult market conditions in 2022 – that the company can do much about other than delivering on the financial forecasts outlined to the investment community. We were very conscious of the need to maintain a high level of engagement and transparency with the investment community and to constantly keep the market informed on the businesses progress.

There are many benefits in being a public company, such as access to capital. There are also significant obligations and responsibilities placed on the business for the privilege. Our strong advice is to 'measure twice and cut once' in making the decision to enter the public company arena. It is not for everyone!

Table 10.1: Judo's history in brief

2015	**Mid 2015:** Judo concept developed
2016	**September 2016:** First office space in Melbourne **Late 2016:** $20m seed funding from family office and management
2017	Built key infrastructure and capabilities ahead of operational launch
2018	**Early 2018:** R1 equity raising $120m One of Australia's largest pre-revenue capital raisings **March 2018:** Official business launch **October 2018:** Sydney office opens
2019	**Early 2019:** Loan book reaches $100m Brisbane office opens **April 2019:** Full banking licence granted by APRA, Judo becomes a bank **May 2019:** Intermediated deposits launch **July 2019:** R2 $400m equity raising Largest private funding round by an Australian start-up **August 2019:** Retail deposits launch **September 2019:** Reached 50 relationship bankers

2020	**January 2020:** $1bn loan book, $1bn deposit book and 164 FTEs **May 2020:** R3 $228m equity raising under backdrop of COVID-19 market disruption **July 2020:** Perth office opens **November 2020:** Adelaide office opens **December 2020:** R4 $284m equity raising, $1.6bn post-money valuation
2021	**March 2021:** First regional office opened in Newcastle **June 2021:** $3.5bn loan book $2.5bn deposit book R5 equity raising $124m, $1.9bn post-money valuation Inaugural Tier 2 issue $50m **October 2021:** Investment grade credit rating issued by S&P **November 2021:** Successful IPO and admission to ASX $2.3bn market cap
2022	**February 2022:** Judo 1H22 Results $4.9bn loan book **May 2022:** Inaugural Investor Day **August 2022:** Judo FY22 Results meet or exceed all prospectus metrics $6.1bn loan book Proforma Profit $15.6m 16 offices open nationally **September 2022:** Inaugural benchmark Public Senior Unsecured issuance **October 2022:** Judo 2022 AGM, $6.8bn loan book

Final reflections

As we put the final touches to this book in late 2022, we are conscious that we all live in highly volatile times. For some, volatility represents dangers; for others, it represents opportunities. Notwithstanding the crisis conditions that engulfed the world in 2022, impacting financial markets and stock valuations, we both believe that the next decade is going to present even stronger opportunities for start-up businesses around the world. With substantial and growing pools of capital around the world looking for strong and innovative new ideas advocated for and led by capable, passionate executives, alongside the continuing huge advances in technology and its affordability, we do see the potential for a golden era of start-ups, which then become unicorns and add greatly to the society in which they operate.

As Joe Giannamore said, we began our entrepreneurial journey as 'no spring chickens'. We were not the 26-year-old corporate rebels suffocating in a world of mind-numbing bureaucracy having spent two years at an expensive business school, or the 20-year-old college dropouts who wanted to be paper billionaires by 25. We are examples of the fact that there is no stereotype to entrepreneurialism. Bill Gates is very different from Richard Branson. The truth is that you are rarely too young, and it is never too late.

Many people who know us will immediately question the discipline with which we follow our own advice. That is not the point.

We made mistakes along the way, but we do not want others to make the same mistakes.

We hope this book, which reflects our personal journey and perspectives on the formative years of Judo Bank, might prove helpful in some small way to the many entrepreneurs out there.

Thanks for reading!

References

Adonis, J, 'This is why entrepreneurs are happier', *The Sydney Morning Herald*, 13 November 2020, smh.com.au/business/small-business/this-is-why-entrepreneurs-are-happier-20201112-p56e0k.html.

Ascher, J & Tonies, F, 'How to turn everyday stress into "optimal stress"', *McKinsey Quarterly*, 18 February 2021, mckinsey.com/capabilities/people-and-organizational-performance/our-insights/how-to-turn-everyday-stress-into-optimal-stress.

Australian Bureau of Statistics, '2071.0.55.001 – Census of Population and Housing: Commuting to Work – More Stories from the Census, 2016, 2016', 25 May 2018, abs.gov.au/ausstats/abs@.nsf/Lookup/by%20Subject/2071.0.55.001~2016~Main%20Features~Feature%20Article:%20Journey%20to%20Work%20in%20Australia~40.

Australian Human Rights Commission, *What's Age Got to Do With It?*, 2021, humanrights.gov.au/sites/default/files/document/publication/ahrc_wagtdwi_2021.pdf.

Baumeister, RF & Tierney, J, *Willpower: Why self-control is the secret to success*, Penguin Books, New York, 2012.

Bersin J & Chamorro-Premuzic, T, 'Age adds the economic edge', *The Australian*, 11 October 2019, theaustralian.com.au/business/careers/age-adds-the-economic-edge/news-story/db409fb36c0b733fb49b29b9f79c4799.

Blank, SG, *The Four Steps to the Epiphany: Successful strategies for products that win*, self-published, California, 2007.

Boden, A, *Banking on It: How I disrupted an industry*, Penguin Random House UK, 2020.

Bryant, PT & Ortiz Terán, E, 'Entrepreneurs' brains are wired differently', *Harvard Business Review*, 19 December 2013, hbr.org/2013/12/entrepreneurs-brains-are-wired-differently.

Christensen, CM, *The Innovator's Dilemma: when new technologies cause great firms to fail*, Harvard Business Review Press, Boston, 1997.

Collins, J, *Good to Great: Why some companies make the leap and others don't*, HarperBusiness, New York, 2001.

Covey, SR, *The 7 Habits of Highly Effective People*, Simon & Schuster, New York, 1989.

Creighton, A, 'Peter Costello's blast at the banks: bring in some competition', *The Australian*, 19 August 2017, theaustralian.com.au/business/financial-services/peter-costellos-blast-at-the-banks-bring-in-some-competition/news-story/97956f0848cff1dfd218b1a272ebe6e7.

Dasey, J, 'Turning 60 is not "end of the road" but ageism in Australia makes life a challenge for new seniors', *ABC News*, 10 April 2022, abc.net.au/news/2022-04-10/ageism-in-australia-turning-60-david-campese-seniors-age-bias/100907090.

Dodgson, M & Gann, D, 'Universities should support more student entrepreneurs. Here's why – and how', The University of Queensland Business School, 16 October 2020, business.uq.edu.au/article/2020/10/universities-should-support-more-student-entrepreneurs-here%E2%80%99s-why-%E2%80%93-and-how.

Drucker, PF, *Innovation and Entrepreneurship: Practice and principles*, Harper & Row, New York, 1985.

Dweck, CS, *Mindset: Changing the way you think to fulfil your potential*, Robinson, London, 2017.

Eisenmann, T, *Why Startups Fail: A new roadmap for entrepreneurial success*, Currency, New York, 2021.

Evans, P & Wurster, TS, *Blown to Bits: How the new economics of information transforms strategy*, Harvard Business School Press, Boston, 2000.

Eyers, J, '$70,000 home loan "loyalty tax" netting banks $4.5b'. *The Australian Financial Review*, 1 August 2022, afr.com/companies/financial-services/70-000-home-loan-loyalty-tax-netting-banks-4-5b-20220729-p5b5m8.

Garratt, B, *The Fish Rots from the Head: The crisis in our boardrooms: developing the crucial skills of the competent director*, HarperCollinsBusiness, 1997.

Gladwell, M, *Blink: The power of thinking without thinking*, Little, Brown & Co., New York, 2005.

id., *David and Goliath: Underdogs, misfits, and the art of battling giants*, Little, Brown & Co., New York, 2013.

id., *Outliers: The story of success*, Little, Brown & Co., New York, 2008.

Gompers, P, Gornall, W, Kaplan, S & Strebulaev, IA, 'How venture capitalists make decisions', *Harvard Business Review*, March–April 2021, hbr.org/2021/03/how-venture-capitalists-make-decisions.

Grieve, C & Kruger, C, 'False promises and the story of Xinja's decision to exit banking', *The Sydney Morning Herald*, 26 December 2020, smh.com.au/business/banking-and-finance/false-promises-and-the-story-of-xinja-s-decision-to-exit-banking-20201224-p56pyf.html.

Hamel, G & Zanini, M, *Humanocracy: Creating organizations as amazing as the people inside them*, Harvard Business Review Press, Boston, 2020.

Hari, J, *Stolen Focus: Why you can't pay attention – and how to think deeply again*, Crown, New York, 2022.

Hayne KM, *Royal Commission into Misconduct in the Banking, Superannuation and Financial Services Industry*, interim report, Commonwealth of Australia, Canberra, 2018.

Healy, J, *Breaking the Banks: What went wrong with Australian banking?*, Impact Press, 2019.

Hebb, DO, *The Organization of Behaviour: A neuropsychological theory*, John Wiley & Sons, New York, 1949.

Immelt, J, *Hot Seat: Hard-won lessons in challenging times*, Hodder & Stoughton, New York, 2021.

Jack, S, 'Lloyds Boss: Mental health issues can break lives', *BBC News*, 22 January 2020, bbc.com/news/business-51201550.

Katzenbach, JR & Smith, DK, *The Wisdom of Teams: Creating the high-performance organization*, Harvard Business School Press, Boston, 1993.

Kepka, A, 'Business startup statistics Australia (2022 update)', *Fundsquire*, 31 August 2020, fundsquire.com.au/business-startup-statistics-australia.

Kim, WC & Mauborgne, RA, *Blue Ocean Strategy*, Harvard Business Review Press, Boston, 2005.

Laing, RD, *The Divided Self: An existential study in sanity and madness*, Tavistock Publications, London, 1960.

Lencioni, P, *The Five Dysfunctions of a Team*, Jossey-Bass, New York, 2002.

MacDonald, N, 'LinkedIn Top Startups 2019: the 25 hottest Australian companies to work for now', LinkedIn, 4 September 2019, linkedin.com/pulse/linkedin-top-startups-2019-25-hottest-australian-work-macdonald/.

Macquarie Wealth Management, *Australian Banks: Computer says yes*, 10 March 2015.

Masters, B, 'Theranos verdict is a cautionary tale for failing entrepreneurs', *Financial Times*, 5 January 2022, ft.com/content/ccaf2dbd-473f-4b1f-8724-79ca735bb07b.

Mavin, D, *The Pyramid of Lies*, Pan Macmillan, 2022.

Mayer, EA, *The Mind-Gut Connection: How the hidden conversation within our bodies impacts our mood, our choices, and our overall health*, Harper Wave, New York, 2015.

Mencken, HL, *Prejudices: Second series*, Borzoi: Alfred A. Knopf, New York, 1920.

Noonan, L, 'Out with the old, in with the new', *Financial Times*, 16 January 2019, ft.com/content/9d5c41f8-18e6-11e9-9e64-d150b3105d21.

O'Hear, S, 'Monzo founder Tom Blomfield is departing the challenger bank and says he's "struggled" during the pandemic', *TechCrunch*, 21 January 2021, techcrunch.com/2021/01/20/enjoying-life-again.

Orwell, G, 'Why I write', *Gangrel*, Summer 1946.

Phillips, EM & Pugh, DS, *How to Get a PhD: A handbook for students and their supervisors*, Open University Press, 1994.

Pink, DH, *Drive: The surprising truth about what motivates us*, Riverhead Books, New York, 2009.

Porter, ME & Kramer, MR, 'Creating shared value: How to reinvent capitalism – and unleash a wave of innovation and growth', *Harvard Business Review*, January–February 2011, hbr.org/2011/01/the-big-idea-creating-shared-value.

Pupkevicius, M, 'What percentage of startups fail: 24 stats and facts for 2022', *Moneyzine*, 28 October 2022, moneyzine.com/startup-resources/what-percentage-of-startups-fail/.

Reynolds, G, 'How exercise could lead to a better brain', *The New York Times Magazine*, 18 April 2012, nytimes.com/2012/04/22/magazine/how-exercise-could-lead-to-a-better-brain.html.

Ries, E, *The Lean Startup: How today's entrepreneurs use continuous innovation to create radically successful businesses*, Crown Business, New York, 2011.

Rojas, CR, 'Eclipse of the public corporation revisited: concentrated equity ownership theory', *Oxford Business Law Blog*, 22 June 2017, blogs.law.ox.ac.uk/business-law-blog/blog/2017/06/eclipse-public-corporation-revisited-concentrated-equity-ownership.

Sapolsky, RM, *Why Zebras Don't Get Ulcers: A guide to stress, stress related diseases, and coping*, W.H. Freeman, New York, 1994.

Schein, EH, *Organizational Culture and Leadership: A dynamic view*, Jossey-Bass, San Francisco, 1985.

Scott, S, *Fierce Conversations: Achieving success at work and in life, one conversation at a time*, Viking, New York, 2002.

Seligman, MEP, *Learned Optimism: How to change your mind and your life*, A.A. Knopf, New York, 1991.

Shi, L, et al., 'Meditation and blood pressure: a meta-analysis of randomized clinical trials', *Journal of Hypertension*, vol. 35, no. 4, 2017, pp. 696–706.

Sinek, S, *Leaders Eat Last: Why some teams pull together and others don't*, Portfolio Penguin, London, 2017.

Smith, A (1776). *An Inquiry into the Nature and Causes of the Wealth of Nations*, W. Strahan and T. Cadell, London, 1776.

Stein Fairhurst, D, *Financial Modeling in Excel for Dummies*, John Wiley & Sons, 2017.

Stephan, U, et al., 'Self-employment and eudaimonic well-being: energised by meaning, enabled by societal legitimacy', *Journal of Business Venturing*, vol. 35, no. 6, 2020, 106047.

Swart, T, Chisholm, K & Brown, P, *Neuroscience for Leadership: Harnessing the brain gain advantage*, Palgrave Macmillan, Hampshire, 2015.

Tavris, C & Aronson, E, *Mistakes Were Made (But Not by Me)*, Harcourt Books, 2007.

The Economist, 'Footloose and fancy-free: retirement is out, new portfolio careers are in', *Special Report: The economics of longevity*, 6 July 2017, economist.com/special-report/2017/07/06/retirement-is-out-new-portfolio-careers-are-in.

id., 'The new old: getting to grips with longevity', *Special Report: The economics of longevity*, 6 July 2017, economist.com/special-report/2017/07/06/getting-to-grips-with-longevity.

id., 'The pandemic could give way to an era of rapid economic growth', 8 December 2020, economist.com/finance-and-economics/2020/12/08/the-pandemic-could-give-way-to-an-era-of-rapid-productivity-growth.

Thiel, P & Masters, B, *Zero to One: Notes on startups, or how to build the future*, Virgin Books, London, 2014.

Wasserman, N, 'The founder's dilemma', *Harvard Business Review*, February 2008, hbr.org/2008/02/the-founders-dilemma.

Wiseman, L, *Multipliers: How the best leaders make everyone smarter*, HarperBusiness, New York, 2017.

Wong, R, 'Finding the right CEO', *Harvard Business Review*, January–February 2022, hbr.org/2022/01/finding-the-right-ceo.

Yoffie, D & Kwak, M, 'Judo strategy: 10 techniques for beating a stronger opponent', *Business Strategy Review*, vol. 13, no. 1, 2002, pp. 20–30.

Zook, C & Allen, J, *The Founder's Mentality: How to overcome the predictable crises of growth*, Harvard Business Review Press, Boston, 2016.

Index

:86 400 89-90
0 to 1 start-up 5, 54, 74, 75
1 to n start-up 5, 54, 75, 89

Abu Dhabi Capital Group (ADCG) 95
Abu Dhabi Investment Council (ADIC) 44
abundant thinking 6, 21-22, 147-148
accountability 39, 136, 137
adrenaline 68-69, 139, 148
advisors 81, 82, 92-95, 180-182
ageism 10-11, 160-163
alcohol 24, 140, 142, 143
Aldermore Bank 20, 22, 27
Alexander, Tim 2, 28, 68, 83, 95
Allen, James 6, 173-174, 175, 177-178
Allison, Jonny 88-89
ambiguity 21, 75, 111-114, 155-156
amygdala 114, 147
AnaCap 22, 155
ANZ Bank 13, 29, 35, 50, 51, 76, 82, 85, 88, 130, 174
Apple 39
Aronson, Elliot 47-48
Ashurst 81, 134, 181
Assaf, Joseph 123
Atom Bank 89
attitude 34
Australia as an investment destination 101, 106-107
Australian Prudential Regulation Authority (APRA) 26, 97, 136

balance 20, 118, 141-142
Baldwin, James 72
Bank of Queensland 83
Banking Executive Accountability Regime (BEAR) 136
banking industry, the 13-17, 25, 39, 41, 56-57, 73, 77, 136
banking licence 26-27, 87, 96-97, 145
Barrenjoey 181
Baumeister, Roy F 148
Bayliss, Chris 2, 29, 43, 68, 83, 94
BC Partners 91
beliefs 40-43, 72, 121
Bell, Robert 89
Bendigo and Adelaide Bank 83
Bertuch, Renée 81
Bishop, Julie 47
black swan events 45, 131
Blank, Steve 61
Blomfield, Tom 115-117, 129, 140-141
blue ocean strategy 59-60, 80
Boden, Anne 138
Boston Consulting Group 73-74
Boutros-Ghali, Boutros 159
brand 67-68
Branson, Richard 185
Brown, Gordon 88
Bryant, Peter T 175
Buckley, Paul 93
Buffett, Warren 23, 149
bureaucracy 73-74, 77, 112-113, 116-117, 120-121, 129, 154, 158-159, 175, 177-178
business model 10, 17-18, 43-45, 48, 54, 61, 63, 65, 73, 79
business plan 37-52, 82

caffeine 140
Callen, Michael 22
Camboova 85, 87, 95
Cameron, David 47
Campbell, Earl 84-85

Cannings Communications 81
capital raising 9-10, 24, 42, 75, 81-107, 159, 166, 179, 185
Cartwright, Peter 22, 46, 155
challenger banks 22, 43, 89, 90, 115
Chartered Banker Institute 122
Cheshire cat 36, 152
cholesterol 73
Christensen, Clayton 32, 56
Chronias, Nick 93
Citibank 181
clarity 37, 41, 104-105
co-CEO model 125-127, 138, 181
cognitive dissonance 31, 47-48, 71-72
collateral 41, 125
Collins, Jim 32, 38, 54, 116
Collins, Megan 29, 110, 119
Colwell, Jacqui 29
Commonwealth Bank of Australia (CBA) 13
competitive advantage 31, 42, 51, 53-54, 57-58, 60-68, 78, 125, 165
complexity 73-74, 117, 175
confirmation bias 33
conflict 126-127, 150-151, 152-153
Connolly, Mickey 152
consistency 39, 98, 102
Conversant 152
Coolidge, Calvin 107, 146
corporate spin 40, 110
cortisol 139, 140
Costello, Peter 17
cost-to-income ratio 56, 76-77
Covey, Stephen R 18, 152
COVID-19 8-9, 35, 46, 75, 96, 101, 102, 131, 159-160
creative thinking 155-156
Credit Suisse 170-172, 181
Credit Suisse Asset Management 95
critical thinking 124-125
cultural capital 28, 109, 136, 178
cultural concrete 14, 135-138, 156, 176
culture 29, 39-40, 53, 62, 65, 67, 68-69, 72, 73, 84, 109-112, 119-120, 122, 130-132, 134-138, 140, 150-151, 156-157, 158, 165, 166, 167, 170, 173-178
customer value proposition 64-65

Dale, Richard 43
data 50, 102, 125
David and Goliath 30-31, 78
Davie, Jonathan 93
Davies, Mervyn 88
Dawes, Seumas 93
decathlon 48-49, 62
del Missier, Jerry 90
Deng Xiaoping 75, 145, 149
diet 143, 163
Dimon, Jamie 174
disruptors 18, 26, 33-34
dividends 20, 26, 180
Donnelly, Martin 93
dopamine 24, 60
Drucker, Peter 38, 79, 104, 135
Dullard, Stuart 81, 181
Dweck, Carol 111

Economist, The 9, 122, 162
ego 47, 117, 148
Einstein, Albert 34
Eisenhower, Dwight 75
Eisenmann, Thomas 8, 102, 166, 167
employee value proposition 49, 110, 122
endorphins 143
Enterprise Rent-A-Car 31-32, 63
entrepreneurs 2, 40, 64, 79, 85, 110, 112-113, 118, 123, 175
—definition 5-6
—perceptions of 67, 185
—pitfalls 7, 30, 45-48, 60-61, 65, 72-74, 117, 119, 129, 133-134, 141, 148

Epictetus 106
equity ownership 132-134, 154-155, 167, 176
Ethnic Business Awards (EBA) 123
Evans, Philip 100

feedback 60, 92
financial modelling 43-44, 76, 82
Financial Services Institute of Australasia (FINSIA) 122
fintech 17, 50, 56, 59, 61, 67, 89
First Avenue Capital Partners 93-94
Fite, David 95
fitness 11, 113, 138-143, 163
flexibility 105-106, 159
Flintoft, James 35
founder centrism 165-178
founder's dilemma 167
founder-led companies 158, 168-172, 174
Frazier, Lisa 63
fundamental attribution error 7

Galbraith, John Kenneth 75
Garcia, Luis 81
Gates, Bill 147, 185
GE Capital 63
General Electric 73
Giannamore, Joe 22-23, 34, 46, 89, 94, 114, 155, 165, 185
giants 30-33, 78
Gladwell, Malcolm 30-31, 60, 78, 121-122, 125
Goldman Sachs 181
Goldwyn, Samuel 93
Gompers, Paul 9
Gordon, Jonathan 81
Greenberg, Jeff 91
Greengate Hotel 13
Greensill Capital 2, 47
Greensill, Lex 47, 148
growth mindset 111
growth, paradox of 74, 158, 175-177

Hamel, Gary 74, 113, 120-121, 154, 158
Hari, Johann 72, 146
Hayne Royal Commission 14, 57, 59, 135-136
Hayne, Kenneth 136
health 11, 113, 138-143, 163
Healy, Joseph vii
Heath, Michael 30, 34
Hebb, Donald 121
Hebbian theory 121
hippocampus 147, 163
Hippocratic Oath 130
Hiscock, Mal 29, 82, 95, 134
homeostasis 139
Hornery, David vii
Horta-Osório, António 138-139
hubris 46-47, 148
hydration 142
hyperbole 71-72

Immelt, Jeff 63, 73, 74, 131, 151
Inception Asset Management 95
influence 14, 130
innovation 32, 56
intrapreneur 6, 10
Ironbridge 87, 95

Jaws ratio 76-77
Jensen, Michael 52
Jiang, Mandy 94-95
Jobs, Steve 110, 112
Jonnola Investments 93
JPMorgan Chase & Co 174
Judo Bank timeline 183-184
judo strategy 31, 78-80
Juneja, Vimpi 43, 78, 156

Katzenbach, Jon R 122
Keenan, Kate 2, 29, 78, 83
Khosla, Rishi 90
Kim, W Chan 80
King's College London 11

Koda Capital 86
Kool-Aid 33, 54
Kraus, Kristofer 91
Kwak, Mary 78

Laing, RD 141
laughter 143
leadership 30, 85, 114, 122, 127-132, 152
learning 1, 121-122, 128, 145, 151
legacy problems 27, 63, 84, 121, 155
Lencioni, Patrick 30, 151
location 31-32, 34-35, 119-120
Leslie, Andrew 181
Lockhart, Gene 90
London 19-20, 22, 24, 91
Lord, Geoff 85
loyalty tax 14

Macquarie Bank 83
Macquarie Bank Equity Research 58
Macy's 103
management 3, 8-9, 11, 19, 42, 66-67, 71, 100, 102, 111, 116-117, 130, 167, 170, 181
market failure 25, 41, 54-59
Marx, Karl 169
massage 143
Mauborgne, Renée 80
Mavin, Duncan 47, 148
McFarlane, John 76, 88, 130, 174
McMurray, Lindsey 90
measure twice, cut once 2, 28, 37-52, 82, 133, 148, 151, 183
meditation 143
Melbourne 34-35, 76, 86
Mencken, HL
mental health 11, 113, 138-143
Metro Bank 89
Mifsud, Steve 110
mindset
—abundant 147-148
—challenger 56, 121, 165-178
—employee 113, 136, 150, 170
—entrepreneurial 110, 118, 170
—equity 132, 134
—founder 1, 67, 110, 121, 158, 165, 168-178
—growth 111
—migrant 123-125, 128, 149, 176
—owner 1, 49, 128, 131, 136, 137, 174
—scarcity 147
Minto, Dylan 20
Moloney, David 43
Monitor Group 51-52
Monks, Phillip 20, 153
Monzo 115, 129, 141
Morgan AO, Dr David 90
Moss, Allan 76
multiplier effect 40
Myer Family Investments 95

naming 77-79
Nangia, Arun 29
National Australia Bank (NAB) 13, 29, 35, 86, 89, 136
neobank 17, 56, 61
Neumann, Adam 148

Obeid, George 30, 34
office space 86-87
Olgers, Kate 81
Olympians 34, 48-49, 62, 79
operating costs 35, 77, 120
optimism 131, 147, 152
OPTrust 95
organisational design 117, 119-121, 154, 167
Orion Corporate Advisory Services 82
Orogen 67
Ortiz Terán, Elena 175
Orwell, George 48
overconfidence 45, 54

Pandit, Vikram 67
Pareto efficiency 25

passion 10, 23-24, 112, 120-121, 150, 154
Pateman, Steve 20, 90, 153
Patterson, Kay 160-161
performance 39, 71, 77, 130, 153, 168, 178
persistence 107, 152
PhD 1
physical health 11, 113, 138-143, 163
Pink, Daniel H 150
Pipilis, Yanni 90
Pitcher Partners 82
Pollen Street Capital, 90, 91
prefrontal cortex 24, 139, 163
problem-solving 131, 146
public listing 96, 101, 166, 173, 179-183
purpose 2, 6, 10, 15, 23-25, 38-40, 63, 110, 112, 126, 147, 150, 151-152, 157, 173
PwC 181

Regus 86
relationships 18, 20, 39, 50, 63, 100, 107, 126, 142, 157-158
remote working 159-160
remuneration 57, 132-134, 154
resilience 11, 35, 105-106, 107, 113, 143, 146, 152
responsibility 47-48, 131, 136
Ries, Eric 60
risk 5-6, 27, 54, 60-61, 66, 72, 102, 119, 129, 133-134
—appetite 6, 99, 114, 118
—generic start-up 45-48
—management 29, 41, 58-60, 65, 101, 118-119
—mini-me 33-34, 40, 67, 68-69, 79, 86, 158, 176-178
—settlement 94
—tail 45, 131
Roberts, William 81
Robinson Crusoe 114-115
Roosevelt, Theodore 146
Royal Commission 14, 57, 59, 135-136
Ruddock, Greg 87, 95

Sapolsky, Robert 140
Scales, Jonathan 93
scaling 68-69, 117-119, 154-155, 165, 175-178
Schein, Edgar 135
Scott, Cécile 29
Scott, Susan 114
self-awareness 140, 143
Seligman, Martin 152
shareholders 20, 153, 180
Shaw, George Bernard 147
Shawbrook Bank 19-20, 22, 27, 90-91
Shorten, Robert 82
Sinek, Simon 112, 138
sleep 138, 140, 142
small- to medium-sized enterprises (SMEs) 15-18, 22-23, 25, 38-39, 41-42, 55, 57-59, 123
Smith, Adam 168-169
Smith, Douglas K 122
social licence 15, 28, 42
Soros, George 91
specialisation 48-49, 62-63, 68, 76
stamina 107, 146
Starling Bank 138
start-ups 2, 5-9
Stileman, David 88
strategy 23, 30-32, 38, 54, 61, 75, 78-80, 89, 135, 155
stress 11, 138-140, 142-143
succession 167-168, 181
sugar 140
Suncorp 83
Swart, Tara 21
Sydney 13, 34-35, 86, 93

Tang Family Office, 95

Tavris, Carol 47-48
Taylor, Jack 31-32
team-building 28-30, 42, 63, 67, 68, 72, 109-138, 149-151, 156-157, 165-166, 168, 181
teamwork 39, 120, 122, 137, 150
technology 46, 50, 61, 65-66, 89-90
Ted Lasso 32
Thiel, Peter 5, 37, 54, 89, 150, 156
Thiel's law 37-38, 60
Thomas, Darrel 30, 34
Thomson, Anthony 89-90
Tierney, John 148
Tikehau Capital 95
Trump, Donald 47, 75
trust 38-39, 110, 126-127, 129, 133, 153
Turnbull, Malcolm 26
Tuszynski, Ben 30, 34
Twigg, Alex 2, 29

uncertainty 15, 74-77
unicorns 6-7, 95-96, 185

values 23, 39-40, 112, 114, 128, 129, 137, 157
VentureCrowd 85, 93
Versace, Frank 30, 34, 58
Vincent Fairfax Family Office 85
vision 2, 6, 10, 18, 31, 38-43, 48-52, 110, 130, 146-148, 151-152, 173
visualisation 34, 85, 146-147, 152

Wanamaker, John 103
Wasserman, Noam 167
Westpac 13
WeWork 2, 148
whiteGREY 81
why, what and how 25-33, 48-52
Wilde, Oscar 158
willpower 147-148
Wiseman, Liz 46-47, 122
Wood, Alison 82
Woodworth, Caroline 90
Wurster, Thomas 100

Xinja Bank 17, 72, 87

Yes, Prime Minister 77
Yoffie, David 78
yoga 143

Zanini, Michelle 74, 113, 120-121, 154, 158
Zhong Yi Investment Pty Ltd 94
Zook, Chris 6, 173-174, 175, 177-178
Zoom 160